Miracle in the Pacific

The Polynesian Cultural Center

Miracle in the Pacific

The Polynesian Cultural Center

Laura F. Willes

DESERET
BOOK

SALT LAKE CITY, UTAH

Photograph and Illustration Credits

All photos are courtesy of the Polynesian Cultural Center and BYU–Hawai`i archives except the following, which are used by permission:

BYU–Provo Photo Archives, pages 9, 10, 59.
Hawai`i Reserve Inc., page 168.
John Muaina, page 165.
LDS Church Archives, pages 13, 116.
Lee Cantwell, page 25.
Martell Gee, page 171.
Ty Jeppesen, page 4.

Library of Congress Cataloging-in-Publication Data

Willes, Laura F., author.
    Miracle in the Pacific : the Polynesian Cultural Center / Laura F. Willes.
        pages   cm
    Includes bibliographical references and index.
    ISBN 978-1-60907-157-8 (hardbound : alk. paper)
    1. Polynesian Cultural Center (Laie, Hawaii)   2. Mormon Church—Hawaii. I. Title.
    BX8643.P635W55 2012
    289.3'969—dc23   2012017144

Printed in Canada
Friesens, Manitoba, Canada

10   9   8   7   6   5   4   3   2   1

Contents

Preface

The Polynesian Cultural Center (PCC) is a forty-two-acre living museum where canoes glide along a freshwater lagoon amid tropical foliage and flowers, and friendly Pacific Islanders in authentic villages share the customs and cultures of their island nations. Guests from all over the world (hundreds of thousands every year) stroll through the villages watching demonstrations of natives climbing coconut trees, throwing spears, starting fires with hibiscus sticks and coconut husks, hosting traditional welcoming ceremonies, beating drums, performing traditional dances, and much, much more.

In the evening, visitors may attend an authentic *luau* (feast) and enjoy the largest Polynesian show in the world, a staged spectacular featuring more than one hundred dancers and musicians. This unique and special place is a microcosm of the fabled South Sea pageant of islands, ocean, and sky.

What visitors to the Polynesian Cultural Center may not realize is that all of these facilities—the beautiful temple on the hill, the Polynesian Cultural Center, and its sister institution, Brigham Young University–Hawai`i (BYU–H)—belong to The Church of Jesus Christ of Latter-day Saints. The university is the realization of a vision that Church leader David O. McKay saw in 1921 when he attended a flag-raising ceremony at the small primary school in Lā`ie, Hawai`i. It took over forty years of dedication and hard work on the part of thousands to make his vision a reality, but BYU–H and the PCC (which grew out of the need for student employment at the college) stand today as a testament to his fortitude and persistence. This is the story of that dream. ❧

Chapter One

Gathering Place

*Re-creation of an early
Polynesian canoe voyage.*

When European sailors first ventured into the Pacific, they were astonished to find a race of people who shared a common cultural heritage and similar languages living on isolated island groups scattered across an area larger than Europe and North America combined. (Later it was discovered that they shared a common genetic heritage too.) Anyone who has flown over or sailed the vast expanses of the Pacific marvels that man ever found and peopled the Pacific Islands.

How they moved from island to island has only recently been understood. What is clear, however, is that these voyagers moved in well-planned expeditions. Their canoes were seaworthy, hydrodynamically advanced, and built for speed, and they carried whole families of men, women, and children to colonize new islands. The travelers were well provisioned, not only with food for the journey, but with seeds, tubers, and cuttings they would need in their new home. Among these were *niu* (coconut), *mai`a* (banana), *ulu* (breadfruit), *kalo* (taro, root vegetable), *uhi* (yam), *ko* (sugarcane), and *wauke* (paper mulberry tree for making tapa, or bark cloth), to name just a few. The canoes also transported dogs, chickens, and pigs. Most important, they were led by experienced and capable navigators.

Having no instruments, charts, or even a written language, the ancient Polynesian navigator plotted his pathway in his mind. The ocean was his highway, and its signs were clear to those who knew the language of the sea. Using sophisticated navigational skills and a prodigious memory, he carefully read the sun, the moon, the stars, the winds, and the behavior of sea birds. In addition, he interpreted the waves and carefully observed the currents, the flotsam and jetsam on the surface, and the moods and feel of the water. With all of these, he could calculate his position on the vast ocean. It is said that a typical navigator had knowledge and recall of up to two hundred different star positions as they rose or set in the sky at any time of year, effectively giving him a star compass in his mind. The Polynesian navigator was really a human Global Positioning System!

These brave voyagers established new settlements wherever they went, bringing with them what they would need for physical survival, as well as the cultural heritage they would pass on to their children. They carefully preserved their genealogies, the deeds of their heroes and heroines, and their history and religion in oral chants and dances. This body of knowledge, which also involved amazing feats of memory, was patiently and carefully passed down through the generations.

Today we know that Polynesia is made up of about three hundred inhabited islands and many other smaller ones that dot the Pacific Ocean, the largest geographic feature on Earth. The term *Polynesia* comes from the Greek words *poly*, meaning "many," and *neso*, meaning "islands." Coined by Charles de Brosses in 1756, the term originally referred to all the Pacific Islands. In 1831, Dumont d'Urville proposed the current, more specific usage, which refers to a group of islands in the western Pacific. D'Urville also introduced the names Melanesia and Micronesia for other regions in the Pacific.

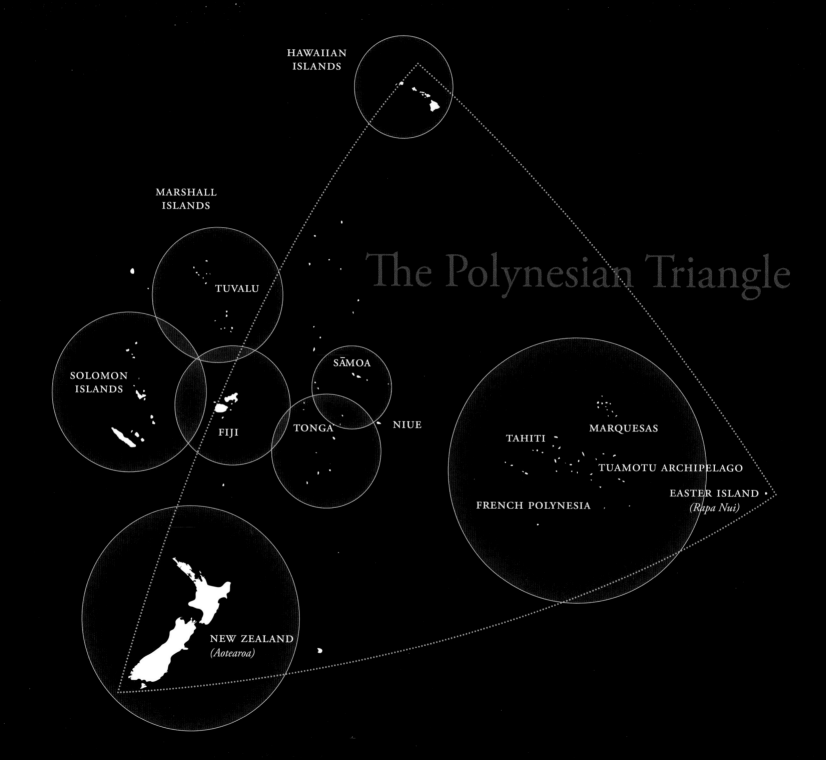

HAWAIIAN
ISLANDS

MARSHALL
ISLANDS

The Polynesian Triangle

TUVALU

SĀMOA

SOLOMON
ISLANDS

FIJI

TONGA   NIUE

MARQUESAS

TAHITI

TUAMOTU ARCHIPELAGO

EASTER ISLAND
(*Rapa Nui*)

FRENCH POLYNESIA

NEW ZEALAND
(*Aotearoa*)

The palm-ruffled borders of Polynesia form a vast aquatic triangle of 15 million square miles, 5,750 statute miles on each side, called the Polynesian Triangle. Hawai`i sits at the northern point of the triangle, Rapa Nui (Easter Island) at the southeastern point, and Aotearoa (New Zealand) anchors the southwest. Included within this geographic area are the nations of Sāmoa (including American Sāmoa and Sāmoa), Tonga, French Polynesia (which includes Tahiti and the Marquesas), Hawai`i, New Zealand, and Easter Island. Fiji lies on the eastern tip of the triangle—part Polynesian, part Melanesian.

Pacific Islands are formed when submarine volcanoes begin to spew magma so hot that fire burns in the dark, cold ocean depths. The layers of magma accumulate slowly, one on top of the other over millennia, until the volcano rises above the waves and continues to climb skyward as a new island. Life arrives on the island on the ocean currents, the jet stream, and as gifts of migratory birds, one new species arriving approximately every 40,000 years. The colonizing plants and animals evolve in complete isolation, making each island a unique and rare biota. Coral reefs often form around the island, providing a habitat for sea life and protection from pounding surf.

This process of geologic island building continues in the Pacific today. Off the coast of the island of Hawai`i, many leagues under the sea, an embryonic island is now glowing with lava flows so hot the sea cannot quench them. The emerging volcano already has a name, Loihi, and two large craters. It is estimated that Loihi will break the ocean surface in about 10,000 years and the Pacific will have yet another island. Some scientists speculate that Loihi may eventually grow higher than Hawai`i's Mauna Kea, the tallest mountain on Earth, as measured from its base on the ocean floor.

Early Hawaiian members of The
Church of Jesus Christ of Latter-day Saints.

Western Contact

Westerners discovered the Polynesian islands in the seventeenth and eighteenth centuries. When English explorer Captain James Cook landed in Hawai`i on January 18, 1778, Hawaiians initially greeted him warmly. But on a subsequent visit, Cook was killed in an altercation at Kealakekua Bay on the Kona coast of the island of Hawai`i. Cook observed the similarities among Polynesian populations separated by great distances in the Pacific, recording in his log that the people of Hawai`i were the same as the people of Tahiti.

The discovery of the Pacific Islands by Westerners excited Europe, and soon explorers were visiting all of them. Whalers, merchants, and missionaries came too. This contact eventually brought changes to the indigenous people in the islands when new ways of life—social, political, religious, and aesthetic—were introduced. The exposure to Western education and literacy, modern agriculture, government, liquor, and diseases for which the Polynesians had no immunity caused them to make thousands of adjustments and changes. The isolated past disappeared, and a new and sometimes baffling future stretched before them.

Missionaries

Protestant missionaries first arrived in Hawai`i in 1820, and Catholic priests came in 1827. For forty years they taught the Polynesians about Jesus Christ, persuading them to forgo their native gods and traditions and become Christian. They taught the women to dress more modestly. *Mu`umu`u* (loose dresses) were created and adopted in Hawai`i, a spinoff of the old Mother Hubbard dresses or nightgowns. The missionaries established schools, learned the native languages, and created written versions of the languages. They taught the people to read and write, and they translated books into the Polynesian languages, the most important being the Old and the New Testaments of the Bible.

LDS Missionaries

In the spring of 1843, only thirteen years after The Church of Jesus Christ of Latter-day Saints was organized, and while the core of Latter-day Saints was settled in Nauvoo, Illinois, the Prophet Joseph Smith, founder of the Church, called four men on missions to the islands of the Pacific. These missionaries, who arrived on the island of Tubai (part of French Polynesia) in 1844, began what has now extended to over 168 years of LDS Church history in the Pacific. This history is as varied as the islands and the people who live there. Missionaries from the Church arrived in Hawai`i in 1850, New Zealand in 1854, Sāmoa in 1888, Tonga in 1891, the Cook Islands in 1899, and Fiji in 1954.

George Q. Cannon was one of the first LDS missionaries sent to Hawai`i. He arrived in 1850.

In 1850 when the first ten LDS missionaries were sent to Hawai`i, they tried unsuccessfully to preach to the *haole* (Caucasian) population. Turning to the Hawaiian natives instead, they found a people who were receptive to their message. The LDS missionaries learned the Hawaiian language, lived with the natives, ate their food, and loved them. Many Hawaiians listened and were baptized. By the end of 1854, there were over four thousand members of The Church of Jesus Christ of Latter-day Saints in Hawai`i.

Lāna`i

At that time, LDS converts, the fruit of far-flung missionary efforts, were encouraged to gather to Zion, or immigrate to the headquarters of the Church in Salt Lake City, Utah. However, a law in the Kingdom of Hawai`i prohibited Hawaiians from emigrating anywhere.

Instead, in 1854, property in the Palawai Basin on the island of Lāna`i was acquired by the Church for an LDS Hawaiian gathering place and named the City of Joseph in the Valley of Ephraim.[1] Hawaiian members were encouraged to move, or gather there, where they could strengthen each other and live the gospel away from the influences of the world. In the beginning, the Lāna`i gathering was seen as a prelude to an eventual move to Zion on the mainland, when laws might become more favorable for such an emigration. However, only 5 percent of the Hawaiian members chose to move to the City of Joseph on Lāna`i.

In 1857, a letter from Brigham Young to the missionaries in Hawai`i and around the world recalled them all to Salt Lake City because a US army was en route to Utah to put down a supposed insurrection by the Mormons. With the elders gone, the mission declined.

Into this leadership void stepped Walter Murray Gibson, who arrived in Hawai`i in 1860. Though a member of the Church with a mission call to Japan from Brigham Young, Gibson saw an opportunity on Lāna`i for his own aggrandizement. He wrote in his journal that he could visualize on Lāna`i a "glorious little kingdom" for himself.[2] Gibson had assumed control on Lāna`i by 1861, collecting money from the Saints to purchase more land, ostensibly for the gathering but putting titles in his own name. He also sold Church memberships and offices (bishops, archbishops, apostles, etc.) to those who could pay, which was against LDS principles.

Three years later, with the "Utah War" resolved, LDS missionaries returned to Hawai`i. Two Apostles, Ezra T. Benson and Lorenzo Snow, accompanied by Elders William W. Cluff, Joseph F. Smith, and Alma Smith (all former missionaries to Hawai`i), also arrived in Honolulu in 1863 to investigate reports of Gibson's unacceptable and unauthorized behavior. By then it was too late for the City of Joseph. The Hawaiian Saints were disillusioned, and many had already left Lāna`i. In 1864, Gibson was excommunicated but refused to hand over the titles and leases to Church property. Thus the Church was defrauded, and the trust of the Hawaiian members was betrayed. The remaining people in the City of Joseph were instructed to leave the island. The Hawaiian Saints were badly demoralized, and many families were without homes or employment.

Lā`ie

In 1864, Elders George Nebeker and Francis A. Hammond were named copresidents of the Hawaiian Mission and arrived in Lā`ie on July 7, 1865. They had been directed by Brigham Young to buy property for a new gathering place. This time, the land would

Lā`ie Church members returning home from Sunday services. Traditionally the women wore white mu`umu`u and woven hats decorated with fresh flowers.

*A stark view of Lā`ie before the
plantation was established in 1864.*

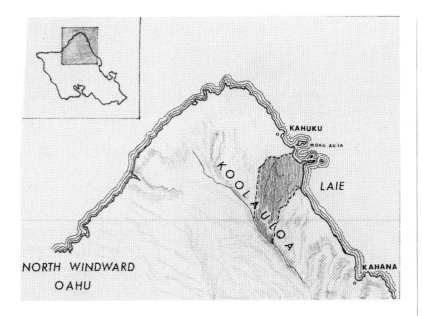

NORTH WINDWARD
OAHU

be completely financed by the Church and used for the good of the Hawaiian Saints, where they could live together for economic benefit, strength, and instruction in gospel living, or "practical salvation,"[3] as Brigham Young called it. Brigham Young advanced $11,515 to the missionaries toward the purchase price of the new gathering place.[4]

A plantation on Oahu was for sale by its owner, Thomas T. Dougherty, and was attractive to Nebeker and Hammond. Named Lā`ie, there was already a small branch of seventy Saints living there. Anciently, Lā`ie had been known as a *pu`uhonua*, or a place of refuge, where transgressors of the law or of the native customs could come to be safe and "cleansed of their transgressions" before returning to society.[5]

The property consisted of two pie-shaped *ahupua`a*[6] (land divisions) which included six thousand acres on the windward side of the north shore of Oahu, nestled between three miles of beach and the Koolau Mountains. Fifteen hundred acres of the land appeared arable. The rest was either mountains or almost-arid plains bordered by the beach. Included in the offer were five hundred head of cattle, five hundred head of sheep, two hundred goats, twenty horses, some farm implements, a large frame house and five Hawaiian houses (all furnished), and several smaller buildings. Five acres of cotton promised to bear a crop, and there were a few patches of land for taro and sweet potato. The asking price was $14,000. Learning that the owner was impatient to sell, Elder Hammond, who was in Hawai`i alone at the time (Nebeker had temporarily returned to Utah to get their families), was in a quandary about what to do. In a day before modern communication, there was no quick way for him to contact Church headquarters for direction. His decision would have to be made without counsel. The answer came in a vivid dream that night when Brigham Young and his counselor, Heber C. Kimball, appeared to Hammond, took him on a survey of the property, and told him that Lā`ie was indeed the chosen spot. Hammond hesitated no longer and bought the property, personally assuming the mortgage of $2,485. There was now a new gathering place called the Lā`ie Plantation. The livestock was sold off to pay Hammond's debt. On November 15, 1879, title to the entire property of Lā`ie was transferred to President John Taylor as Trustee-in-Trust of the Church.[7]

In addition to its significance to Hawai`i, the Lā`ie Plantation can be seen as the first important step toward the establishment of a worldwide Church. Some overlook this development because Hawai`i is now a state, but in 1865 it was a foreign monarchy. The fact that Church leaders established the first gathering place outside the Intermountain West of the United States in what was a foreign country, just a few years after the pioneers entered the Salt Lake Valley, is significant.

But the Lāʻie of today bears little resemblance to the desolate coastal plain that the elders found waiting for them. Sweeping back from the beach and the grasslands, the land rose in a long coastal slope that had been ruthlessly denuded by grazing cattle. The plantation developed slowly but with great effort and industry on the part of the leaders and the Saints who moved there.

Brigham Young sent additional haole missionaries to help run the plantation. The settlers divided the land and built homes. Some Hawaiians constructed frame houses, but most lived in traditional grass huts. The Church owned the land and did not ask for financial support from the Hawaiians. Instead, land was rented to the Hawaiians on a share basis, and each family was loaned enough for a home and garden, with nominal rent. Most of the acreage was planted in sugarcane, and eventually milling equipment was installed for the benefit of the whole plantation. An elementary school was established. This small school was taught by the missionaries for many years and would play a significant role in 1921 (see chapter 2). Later, the school was turned over to the Territory of Hawaiʻi and became a public school.

Problems plagued the plantation during the first decades. Salty winds blew constantly over the north end of the island, making it difficult to grow crops. More serious was an insufficient supply of water, and several disastrously dry years were experienced. The settlers became discouraged at the slow progress of the plantation, and many considered leaving. A meeting was called to discuss the matter. President Joseph F. Smith, counselor in the LDS First Presidency who was in Hawaiʻi on his third mission (1885–87), rose to address the people. As a fifteen-year-old, Joseph F. Smith had served a mission among the Hawaiians. Called Iosepa (Joseph) by the people, he was well known and greatly beloved.

"My brothers and sisters," he began. "Do not leave this land, for this place has been chosen by the Lord as a gathering place for the Saints of The Church of Jesus Christ of Latter-day Saints in *Hawaiʻi nei*. Do not complain because of the many trials which come to you because of the barrenness of the land, the lack of water, the scarcity of foods to which you are accustomed, and poverty as well. Be patient, for the day is coming when this land will become a most beautiful land. Water shall spring forth in abundance, and upon the barren land you now see, the Saints will build homes, taro will be planted, and there will be plenty to eat and drink. Many trees will be planted and . . . the fragrance of flowers will fill the air and trees which are now seen growing on the mountains will be moved by the Saints and will grow in this place near the sea, and because of the great beauty of the land, birds will come here and sing their songs. . . . Therefore, do not waver, work with patience, continue on, stand firm, keep the commandments and . . . you will receive greater blessings . . . than you now enjoy or have enjoyed in the past."[8] His words gave the discouraged Saints reassurance to carry on. In later years, the Lāʻie Plantation developed in almost precisely the manner in which President Smith had foreseen.

Around the turn of the century, the plantation got a new boost when Samuel E. Woolley was called as mission president. He arrived in 1885 to start a mission that lasted almost twenty-five years. Progress on the plantation had been static because the land would not provide a living for more than ninety to one hundred employees. But Woolley enlarged the acreage under cultivation, enabling the population of Lāʻie to gradually grow. By the early 1920s there were nearly a thousand residents.

Critical to this progress was the increased availability of fresh water. In 1881, the first well was drilled in Lāʻie by a Chinese lease holder, successfully tapping into reserves of fresh water accumulated from rain under the cap rock. A year later three artesian wells were flowing. In 1898, Woolley installed a steam-powered water pump and added more over the years, until by 1930 the plantation had a capacity to pump eight million gallons of water daily to the thirsty fields. From 1900 until the early 1920s, the plantation paid its own way every year.

Lāʻie was never the center of the Latter-day Saint population in Hawaiʻi, where membership was spread over all the islands. For the first fifty-four years, the headquarters of the Hawaiʻi Mission was in Lāʻie, but in 1919, both the mission home and mission office were moved to Honolulu. By then the Church in Hawaiʻi had ten thousand members and forty-six missionaries, and Honolulu was the center of the greatest concentration of Mormons in the state, as well as the most convenient transportation hub and the center of Church activities. But since 1865, Lāʻie always was, and continues to be today, the spiritual center of the Church in Hawaiʻi. Lāʻie "occupies a place in the hearts of the Hawaiian Saints," many of whom are descendants of the original Latter-day Saint converts, similar to their feelings for Salt Lake City,[9] the headquarters of the Church. It is the "home place" of the Church in Hawaiʻi.

LĀʻIE TEMPLE

Building a temple in the Hawaiian Islands had been the dream of many devoted and faithful Saints since the restored gospel first came to Hawaiʻi in 1850, and had been prophesied on several occasions.[10] LDS doctrine teaches that without the ordinances of the temple—families sealed together for eternity, and vicarious baptism for dead relatives who did not have this blessing in life—our spiritual lives are incomplete. To be effective, these ordinances must be performed by one holding priesthood authority, in a specially dedicated and hallowed temple. At the turn of the twentieth century

Affectionately called Iosepa *(Joseph) by the Hawaiian people, Joseph F. Smith first came to Hawaiʻi as a teenage missionary.*

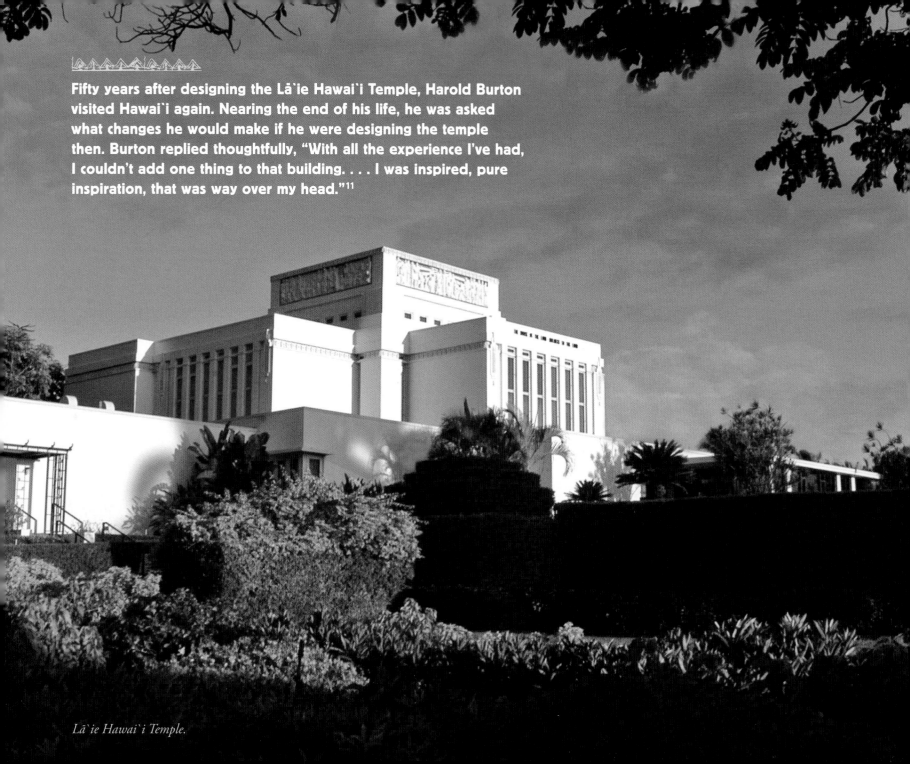

Fifty years after designing the Lāʻie Hawaiʻi Temple, Harold Burton visited Hawaiʻi again. Nearing the end of his life, he was asked what changes he would make if he were designing the temple then. Burton replied thoughtfully, "With all the experience I've had, I couldn't add one thing to that building. . . . I was inspired, pure inspiration, that was way over my head."[11]

Lāʻie Hawaiʻi Temple.

the Church had only four temples in the world, all in Utah.[12] So strong was the desire to attend a temple that some Hawaiians even left the islands and moved to Utah to be near the Salt Lake Temple. They settled in the high desert country of Skull Valley, named their settlement Iosepa (after Joseph F. Smith), and struggled valiantly against the mountain air, freezing winters, parched summer heat, language barriers, and homesickness.

On June 1, 1915, Joseph F. Smith, then President of the Church, was prompted while visiting Lā`ie to dedicate ground for a new temple, and he did so with a rich spiritual outpouring. This came as a surprise to everyone. Apostle Reed Smoot, who witnessed the unexpected event in Lā`ie that day, said, "Never in all my life did I hear such a prayer. The very ground seemed to be sacred, and [President Smith] seemed as if he were talking face to face with the Father. I cannot and never will forget it if I live a thousand years."[13] Planning and construction moved immediately ahead. However, Joseph F. Smith died on November 19, 1918, and did not live to see the completion of the temple.

When plans for the Lā`ie Temple were announced, Polynesian members throughout the Pacific rejoiced and began saving their money and making preparations to travel to Lā`ie to receive their ordinances. In Utah, the town of Iosepa was largely abandoned, and most of its residents returned to Hawai`i to support the construction and work of the new temple.

The official groundbreaking for the temple was held in early February 1916, but construction was not completed for three years. Designed by architects Hyrum C. Pope and Harold W. Burton, who at age twenty-nine was just starting his career, the temple is built in the form of a Grecian cross, measuring one hundred feet by seventy-eight feet. Originally it provided 10,500 square feet of space, which was adorned with large murals by artist LeConte Stewart and others. The temple has no towers or steeple but rises as a monolith to a height of fifty feet. It is tooled to a white cream finish and is adorned around the top with scriptural friezes by sculptors Leo and Avard Fairbanks. Built with Hawaiian labor and skill, it was constructed with steel and local crushed lava rock, and

LEFT: *Construction of the Lā`ie Hawai`i Temple.*
ABOVE: *Church members gather in 1963 around a pool that forms part of the temple landscaping.*

coral aggregate was used to make the concrete. The foundation was dug through soil and coral to a depth of fifteen feet. Hawaiian members raised $60,000 of the $250,000 needed for construction.

Sitting on a hill, white and majestic, with an unobstructed view of the Pacific Ocean, the Lā`ie Temple is a jewel, recognized as one of the most beautiful buildings in Hawai`i. Landscaped with trees, shrubs, flowers, concrete walks, and three oblong pool terraces descending the gentle slope toward the Pacific, the temple presents a truly breathtaking picture. Upon completion the temple became, and remains, a major tourist attraction. Some have referred to it as the Taj Mahal of the Pacific.

When the temple was dedicated on Thanksgiving Day 1919, by President Heber J. Grant, it was the fifth temple completed by the Church (after its arrival in Utah), and the first built outside the continental United States.[14] Over three hundred members, including all the full-time missionaries, were admitted to the temple, upon written recommendation, to witness the dedicatory services.

Changes by 1950

After Western contact, the native Hawaiian population was in decline, struck down especially by maladies for which they had no immunity. By 1900, native Hawaiians had fallen to one-fourth of the total population of Hawai`i and would never again be a majority.[15] Still, until 1920, the Church in Hawai`i consisted mostly of Hawaiian members. Church services were all conducted in Hawaiian, as were sessions in the Lā`ie Temple. The Honolulu Branch, with 891 members, was probably the largest branch of the Church outside Utah at that time, and by 1920 there were over 11,000 LDS members in Hawai`i.

Economically, the Hawaiian Islands made great progress between 1865 and 1895, and the population changed significantly. Hawai`i became a sugar source for the United States but suffered from a labor shortage. Plantation owners and government officials found it necessary to go outside the islands for additional workers. In 1864, the government organized the Bureau of Immigration to facilitate this process. By the end of 1865, 1,306 Chinese contract workers had come to Hawai`i. Three years later, about 150 Japanese workers were brought in. As the native population declined, the foreign population grew and increased steadily for the next two decades. By 1890, when the total population of Hawai`i reached 90,000, over 55,000 were laborers born in foreign countries, coming from such diverse places as China, Japan, Portugal, the Philippines, and Korea. The haole population also grew rapidly, especially after World War II. This trend continues, and today Hawai`i is among the most culturally and ethnically diverse states in the Union. The town of Lā`ie is even more so. The 2000 United States census showed that the Lā`ie population came from a more diverse ethnic background than any other community in the state. In a culturally diverse state, Lā`ie is the most diverse community of all. Hawai`i became a true melting pot, where to this day, no one ethnic group holds a majority. These population trends are also reflected in the LDS Church population, which became a melting pot too.

Governmentally, the Kingdom of Hawai`i was replaced in 1893 with the Hawaiian Republic, bringing an end to the monarchy. In 1898, an act passed in Washington DC called for annexation of the islands as a territory of the United States. Two years later, on June 14, 1900, Hawai`i officially became a territory of the United States, and, almost sixty years later in 1959, it was made the fiftieth state in the Union. 🌾

Chapter Two

No Ordinary College

Traveling companions David O. McKay and Hugh J. Cannon in Polynesian dress.

Hugh J. Cannon and David O. McKay on their 1921 trip to the missions of the world.

By 1920, the Church had been sending missionaries to many parts of the world for over eighty years. Many converts had gathered to Utah, but that practice was now being discouraged, and people were asked to stay in their home countries, where they were organized into congregations often presided over by missionaries. Before modern communication and travel, contact between the missions and the headquarters of the Church in Salt Lake City was minimal, except in America and Europe.

Many of the far-flung congregations had never seen a General Authority,[1] and could not rely on regular direction from Church headquarters. Even more critical, Church leaders in Salt Lake City sometimes lacked full understanding of the unique problems members faced in their individual countries.

President Heber J. Grant took measures to rectify this situation when, in October 1920, he called Apostle David O. McKay to visit all the missions in the Pacific and assess their special needs, the first time this had ever been done. Elder McKay was authorized to extend his trip to other missions if he felt it advisable. David O. McKay was then a young Apostle, but he would subsequently serve forty-four years in the Quorum of the Twelve Apostles and nineteen years as President of Church. Accompanied by President Hugh J. Cannon,[2] president of the Liberty Stake in Salt Lake City, Elder McKay started his trip in Asia and then progressed to all of the missions in the Pacific. He opted to continue to other countries, and the trip turned into a year-long circumnavigation of the globe covering 67,819 miles by water (over every ocean in the world except the Arctic) and 24,277 miles by land.

The five months Elders McKay and Cannon spent traveling in Polynesia were probably the most spiritually compelling of the whole journey. Experiences included an incident at the Pulehu Chapel on Maui when George Q. Cannon and Joseph F. Smith (deceased fathers of two of the men at the meeting) were seen shaking hands in a vision of Brother Keola Kailimai during a prayer, signaling their approval of the event; and a visit to Kilauea, the volcano on the island of Hawai`i, where David O. McKay and his companions were miraculously warned and barely escaped death when the ledge on which they had been standing fell into the fiery crater.

Their experiences included a *hui tau* (annual gathering) in New Zealand in which the gift of interpretation of tongues was fully active for all as Elder McKay spoke to the Māori Saints and was understood perfectly without an interpreter, and the spiritually charged farewell by the Samoan Saints at Saniatu when Elder McKay gave them a blessing by the authority he held as an Apostle of Jesus Christ. But no event cast a longer shadow into the future than when Elders McKay and Cannon attended a flag-raising ceremony at the small elementary school in Lā`ie.

Flag-raising ceremony at the Lā`ie primary school that inspired David O. McKay.

They arrived in Honolulu in February 1921, the first stop on their tour of the Polynesian missions. They traveled thirty-five miles to the north shore of Oahu to visit the Lā`ie Plantation, which had been functioning for over fifty years as the Hawaiian gathering place, and where the new temple stood, dedicated just fourteen months previously.

They especially wanted to visit the Lā`ie elementary school, which was maintained by the mission. This visit would prove to be one of the most significant events of Elder McKay's journey. There was great excitement to welcome an Apostle to the small school. In the early morning, 127 barefoot children, ranging in age from seven to fourteen, lined up expectantly to greet their special visitors.

When all was in readiness, William Ka`a`a, a full-blooded Hawaiian, stepped from the ranks declaring:

> *Hats off!*
> *Along the street there comes*
> *A blare of bugles,*
> *A ruffle of drums,*
> *A splash of color beneath the sky,*
> *Hats off! The flag is passing by.*

Then Thomas Waddoups, a young haole, spoke:

> *Now raise the starry banner up,*
> *Emblem of our country's glory,*
> *And teach the children of this land*
> *Its grave and wondrous story;*
> *Of how in early times it waved*
> *High o'er the Continentals,*
> *Who fought and made our country free,*
> *The one true home of liberty.*

As the flag was raised to its place atop the flagpole, a Japanese boy, Otokochi Matsumoto, came forward:

> *Salute the flag, oh children,*
> *With grave and reverent hand,*
> *For it means far more than the eye can see,*
> *Your home and your native land.*
> *And many have died for its crimson bars,*
> *Its field of blue with the spangled stars.*

At the conclusion of this verse, all who were present, children and adults, saluted the flag and repeated in unison the Pledge of Allegiance. Then William Ka`a`a concluded the ceremony:

> *This flag that now waves o'er our school,*
> *Protecting weak and strong,*
> *Is the flag that vindicates the right*
> *And punishes the wrong.*[3]

Visibly touched, Elder McKay later wrote in his journal that the flag-raising ceremony was "a most impressive and inspiring sight."[4] He noted, "As I looked at that . . . group of youngsters . . . all thrown into . . . the 'Melting Pot' and coming out Americans, my bosom swelled with emotion and tears came to my eyes and I felt like bowing in prayer and thanksgiving for the glorious country which is doing so much for all these nationalities. But more than that . . . I realize that these same boys and girls have the opportunity of participating in all the blessings of the Gospel which will transform [them] into real citizen[s] of the Kingdom of God. I feel to praise His name for the glorious privileges vouch-safed to this generation."[5] Elder McKay went on to record that short services were held in the schoolroom after the flag-raising ceremony "in which all—American, Hawaiian, Japanese, Chinese, Filipino—participated as though they . . . belonged to one nation, one country, one tongue." He concluded, "The Church of Christ will truly make of all nations one blood. May God hasten the day when this is accomplished."[6]

Elder McKay had seen the future. He would hold in his mind the vision of the flag-raising ceremony and the unifying power of the gospel to unite all peoples of the world. But more than that, he would work tenaciously to make it happen. Almost thirty-five years later, in a seeming sudden burst of activity, not one but two institutions, linked in purpose, would be born in the same decade that would change Lā`ie forever. The first long-anticipated development was the establishment of a college.

Education and the LDS Church

Since its organization by Joseph Smith in 1830 in Fayette, New York, The Church of Jesus Christ of Latter-day Saints had been establishing schools, both public and private, and had strongly supported education. In Nauvoo, where the Saints were gathered from 1839 to 1846, a system of education was established under the authority of the Nauvoo Charter granted by the state of Illinois, and it included a university. Even after the Saints were driven from Nauvoo by mobs and trekked across the plains as pioneers to establish themselves in Utah, groups of children and adults were regularly called together for study and instruction. In Utah a small school was taught in 1847 by Mary Jane Hammond in a tent amid the vast wilderness surrounding the Great Salt Lake, within weeks after the first pioneers arrived in the valley.[7] As the population in Utah grew, schools were organized in each congregation. This pattern continued wherever the Saints settled and extended to various areas of the world where LDS

missionaries were active and where local infrastructure did not provide such opportunities.

During the 1940s and early 1950s, the Church recognized the urgent need for schools in the Pacific Islands. The Liahona College in Tonga (started in 1948), the Church College of Western Sāmoa, the Church College of New Zealand near Hamilton, and several elementary schools in these same countries were opened. Even though three of these schools were called "colleges," they included instruction on only a secondary or high school level. A true college in the Pacific was still desperately needed so students coming out of these other institutions could complete their higher education.

Apostle David O. McKay continually advocated establishing such a school. In 1941, as a counselor in the First Presidency, he returned to Hawai`i to dedicate the Honolulu Tabernacle on Beretania Street. In his remarks that day, he reminded the Saints of the goal for a true college. Even though the Church had a fine new tabernacle and a dozen or more beautiful chapels in Hawai`i, he cautioned, "Don't forget Lā`ie. This is the educational center and the spiritual center of our people in these islands."[8]

The Church College of Hawai`i Announced

By the early 1950s, The Church of Jesus Christ of Latter-day Saints was well established in Hawai`i, where it had been making converts and organizing congregations for a hundred years. In 1951, there were sixteen wards and branches and eleven thousand members on Oahu alone, all organized as the Oahu Stake. In April of that same year, David O. McKay became President of the Church. Now a new college in Hawai`i seemed more probable. Members in Hawai`i and in Salt Lake City thought the college would surely be located in Honolulu where a majority of the Saints lived, and certainly no farther away than Kaneohe. But President McKay never wavered in his belief that the college would be built in Lā`ie.

On July 7, 1954, an official announcement by the First Presidency came via radio, television, and newspaper that the Church would establish a two-year college in Lā`ie, Hawai`i, for the young people of the Pacific. The college was projected to open in September 1955, just fourteen short months away. Dr. Reuben Law, then dean of the College of Education at Brigham Young University in Provo, was chosen to be its first president. Dr. Law and his party left immediately for Hawai`i and were welcomed six days later in Honolulu where *lei* were piled to the top of their ears in true Hawaiian fashion.

Dr. Law's assignment in Hawai`i was monumental—start a new college literally from nothing, and do it in fourteen months. There was no campus, no faculty, no students seeking enrollment, and no academic calendar. There was not one book in the library; in fact, there was no library. There was nothing, except an empty sugarcane field sitting in the warm Hawaiian sunshine in the little town of Lā`ie on the north shore of Oahu. The proposed two-year institution didn't even have a name. But that was soon remedied when the First Presidency recommended that it be called the Church College of Hawai`i (CCH).

Dr. Law and the Continuing Advisory Committee called by President McKay (later called the Board of Trustees) set to work. Members included Edward LaVaun Clissold, president of the Oahu Stake;[9] Ralph E. Woolley, former president of the Oahu Stake; and D. Arthur Haycock, then president of the Hawaiian Mission. George Q. Cannon Jr. and Lawrence Haneberg were later invited to join the board.

On November 23, 1954, the Continuing Advisory Committee tackled a lengthy list of critical items. After long and earnest debate, they reached one final decision—they couldn't possibly make President McKay's projected opening date. The college would have to open a year later, in September 1956 instead of 1955. This recommendation was included in their written report.

Three months later, Dr. Law personally placed the report on President McKay's desk in Salt Lake City. The president studied it carefully, nodding his head with approval. But when he came to the last paragraph, which recommended opening the college one year later, he was concerned. Dr. Law explained that, among other things, drawings and blueprints for permanent buildings couldn't be processed in Hawai`i that quickly. The committee, he said, deemed it unwise to open prematurely with a half-finished campus. President McKay's expression was serious. "Oh! We have waited too long already to establish that college. We must start this fall even if we have to start in temporary quarters."[10] The projected opening day would stay as it had been announced from the beginning, September 1955, just nine months away.

Now the challenge was even greater. Not only must work move forward quickly on a permanent campus, but a temporary campus must also be built. The decision was made to locate the temporary campus at the foot of temple hill in Lā`ie by the existing chapel, which could then be utilized for assemblies and other purposes. Clissold, chairman of the Continuing Advisory Committee, took over responsibility for the temporary campus. By mid-March he had located and purchased a dozen vacant cottages in Honolulu and arranged to have flatbed trucks move the cottages along two-lane Kamehameha Highway to Lā`ie. Early in April, four war surplus barracks at Wheeler Air Force Base were acquired. Carpenters sawed the barracks into sections, and by the end of the month they too were headed north. To avoid obstructing traffic, the trucks moved only between midnight and dawn. For several weeks, daytime motorists

Temporary campus that served as the Church College of Hawai`i for three years.

saw the sections resting beside the highway, parked until the countryside went to bed. At one time there were sixteen sections of buildings moving to Lā`ie. Once there, they were remodeled, repaired, renovated, and painted by a crew of workmen under the direction of bishops Russell Robertson and Kuailipo`ilani (Po`i) Kekauoha. By September, the workers had done the impossible, and a temporary campus clustered around the chapel with a library, dormitory, cafeteria, and several classrooms. Grass was even growing around the buildings, and all was in readiness.

Meanwhile, throughout the spring and summer, architectural plans for the permanent campus were being reviewed and the 1955–56 academic calendar had final approval. Prospective faculty members were being hired and inquiries were coming in from persons seeking office, faculty, and maintenance jobs. In addition, high school students all over Hawai`i were being recruited. By the end of February the first student had been admitted—Glen Auna from Honoka`a on the island of Hawai`i. He was so excited that he arrived in Lā`ie two weeks before the CCH opened. By September, 153 eager men and women had been enrolled, most of them from the Hawaiian Islands. There had been little time to recruit students from other island nations, but that would change dramatically in the future.

The original twenty faculty members were brought together from many institutions and locations, but they cooperated well in achieving a feeling of unity. The last faculty members arrived on September 15, a week before school opened. These families swelled the population of Lā`ie and were warmly welcomed in true Hawaiian fashion. Morale was high, and a spirit of anticipation and excitement prevailed. On September 28, the faculty and student body sat down at their new desks for the fall term. The Church College of Hawai`i was open for learning.

Groundbreaking for the Permanent Campus

As feverish work on the temporary campus went on, plans were being drawn up and approved for the permanent campus to rise on a cane field southeast of the temporary campus. Harold W. Burton of Los Angeles was selected in November 1954 as architect for the college.

In early 1955, President McKay was scheduled to fly to Polynesia, and the groundbreaking for the CCH's permanent campus was added as the climax on his agenda. On the appointed day, February 12, 1955, a small group of Saints gathered at a temporary platform in the cane field. It had been overcast and raining hard all morning. A brief conversation took place between President McKay and his traveling companion, Franklin Murdock, in the car as they pulled into the cane field. Murdock recalled the incident: "'President McKay, you're not going out in this downpour, are you?' President McKay answered unhesitatingly, 'Come on; where's your faith?'

Groundbreaking ceremonies for the Church College of Hawai'i.
FRONT ROW, LEFT TO RIGHT: *Clifford E. Young, Laurence Haneberg,*
D. Arthur Haycock, Edward L. Clissold, President David O. McKay,
Ralph E. Woolley, George Kekauoha, Benjamin M. Bowring.

Then he opened the door and stepped out. As he did so, the rains ceased and the sun came out."[11]

Dr. Law spoke, assuring the audience that this groundbreaking would go down in memory as a source of inspiration for the things that were to come. His comments proved true. The groundbreaking was a rich spiritual outpouring, which is referenced and remembered even today at BYU–H and the PCC.

When President McKay came to the microphone, it was the first time he had stood before a congregation in Lā`ie since becoming President of the Church in 1951. He reminded everyone of his long-held vision for Lā`ie. "This is the beginning of the realization of a vision I saw thirty-four years ago when . . . I witnessed a flag-raising ceremony by students of the Church school here . . . in Lā`ie," he said. It was then that "we visualized the possibilities of making this the center . . . of the education of the people of these islands. . . . I have always cherished the memory of the vision of that morning."[12]

Then President McKay went on to talk of the future. "The world needs men who cannot be bought or sold, . . . genuine gold," he said. "That is what this school is going to produce. . . . You mark [my] word," he continued, "[that] from this school . . . will go men and women whose influence will be felt for good towards the establishment of peace internationally."[13] He noted that the Church was small, only 1,350,000 members, "but oh how those members, . . . who are true to the ideals, will leaven the whole lot."[14] Following the talks, the group moved off the platform, and President McKay turned over the first shovelful of earth.

He was not finished, though, with his vision for Lā`ie's future. In the stirring dedicatory prayer, President McKay articulated a transcendent new vision, which anticipated the development of the Polynesian Cultural Center. He prayed "that this college, and the temple, and the town of Lā`ie, may become a missionary factor, influencing not thousands, not tens of thousands, but millions of people, who will come seeking to know what this town and its significance are."[15]

Labor Missionaries

Work on the permanent campus proceeded with a very unique labor force. President McKay had requested that the Labor Missionary Program, which had been so successful in other parts of the Pacific in recent years, build the CCH's permanent home.

Historically, Mormons had built their public buildings, even the great tabernacle and temple in Salt Lake City, Utah, with their own hands. But over time this practice changed, and contractors and skilled labor began to do much of the construction for the Church, although members were sometimes given the opportunity to help where they could.

During his 1921 world tour, Elder McKay had observed young Māori men who were called to help build a school in New Zealand when no other labor was available. He learned that they had known nothing about the particular building trade they were engaged in before their call. This experience convinced him that similar projects could be started with properly supervised untrained labor, not only in the Pacific, but in Europe and South America, where the need for Church buildings was great. He saw clearly that this would not only benefit Church infrastructure, but would train many young men in useful careers.

Thus began a gigantic building project unparalleled in Church history and initiated the policy of calling members to serve as construction or labor missionaries. The Labor Missionary Program was headed by Wendell B. Mendenhall,[16] who saw the program as a restoration of the Church's pioneer-era building efforts. The

Sign erected by the labor missionaries at the end of construction in 1958.

THE
CHURCH COLLEGE
OF HAWAII
BUILT BY
LABOR MISSIONARIES
THE CHURCH OF JESUS CHRIST OF LATTER-DAY SAINTS
THRIFT AND INDUSTRY

program spread to Europe and Latin America and was responsible for the construction of some two thousand buildings.

On each project, skilled professional supervisors were called, most of them from the US mainland. Each was asked to interrupt his career, uproot his family, and move thousands of miles to a construction site. Young labor missionaries were called to do exactly the same thing. That they all did this willingly, even eagerly, is a testament to their deep commitment and dedication to the gospel of Jesus Christ.

In this way, young labor missionaries could serve their two-year missions for the Church as building missionaries. They would personally realize many blessings for this service, including learning English and gaining expert, on-the-job training as masons, carpenters, plumbers, and electricians—trades they would often follow for the rest of their lives. What became clear only years later was that through this program, the Church, which does not have a paid clergy, would benefit by getting a seasoned and schooled generation of leaders who for decades would ably lead LDS congregations all over the Pacific. It was a win-win situation all around.

President McKay now called on the Pacific labor missionary system for volunteers to finish the job at Lā`ie. On July 21, Joseph E. Wilson, a large-scale contractor from Englewood, California, was chosen as general superintendent. He was in Hawai`i ten days later to assume his duties, even though he and his wife had just completed a new home in California. Over 150 supervisors and young missionaries eventually followed him to Lā`ie as labor missionaries.

As the missionaries began to work, they discovered that the red earth of Lā`ie was soft, spongy, and unable to bear the weight of the planned buildings. To solve the problem, 75,000 cubic yards of coral was blasted out of a pit behind the campus, put through a rock crusher, and laid down two feet deep over the entire site as a foundation for the buildings. For the next three years the labor missionaries toiled, pouring the massive precast concrete wall panels and then swinging them into place with cranes.

During their arduous three-year task the missionaries did not waver. They knew that they were engaged in a long, grueling, and glorious task. They saw the gleaming new school buildings as monuments to the gospel, as well as to their own personal testimonies. They contributed almost 280,000 man-hours of labor without pay, and built for the Church a $3,580,000 campus, a "beacon college of the Pacific," as it was often called. It was estimated they had saved the Church $1,300,000. Without the great gift of their labor and dedication, the CCH would not exist.

Dedication of the Church College of Hawai`i

Eighty-five-year-old President of the Church David O. McKay and his wife, Emma Ray, came to Lā`ie for the dedication services. Other dignitaries in attendance were the governor of Hawai`i, the mayor of Honolulu, and the state superintendent of education. It would be President McKay's last trip to Hawai`i, although no one knew it at the time. His posture was still erect, and his white wavy hair was tousled by the cooling trade winds. He walked at the head of a delegation down Kulanui Street as school children held garlands of flowers across the street and swung them aside as his entourage passed. A thousand townspeople and guests filled the auditorium, which could not contain all those who wished to attend. Two thousand more overflowed into nearby classrooms and stood on the grounds outside. To President McKay's delight, the famous 1921 flag-raising ceremony was reenacted by Lā`ie school children. The first eleven rows of the auditorium were reserved for the labor missionaries, front row and center.

President David O. McKay dedicates the Church College of Hawaiʻi's permanent campus in 1958.

Wendell Mendenhall paid tribute to the labor missionaries and their families at the dedication: "When I see men out there who have sold their own personal belongings to keep two or three sons in the Church missionary field while they, the fathers, were working here on this college; when I see men who have actually lost their homes while working as labor missionaries on this school; when I see the local families who have sent their boys to us to help out, though they were needed at home—when I see that kind of devotion and loyalty to the doctrines of this Church and to the edict to build this school . . . I tell you, students, you are walking on hallowed ground, before you ever step into a single classroom!"[17]

Commendation was given to the wives of the labor missionaries, to the women of Lāʻie, and to many students, who had thrown their whole-hearted support to the project, laying 150,000 square feet of floor tiles in the buildings, washing all the windows and, in

LDS Church President David O. McKay and his wife, Emma Ray, are greeted island style.

many instances, working alongside the men in whatever capacity they were needed.

At the dedication, Edward Clissold recounted the long chain of spiritual events leading up to the college. "We believe that God's purposes began to unfold when this land was chosen by W. W. Cluff [in 1865],"[18] he said, and went on to talk about Joseph F. Smith's prophecy and blessings on Lāʻie, the inspired dedication of the temple site in 1915, and its completion in 1919. He spoke of David O. McKay's experience at the flag-raising ceremony and his subsequent vision of a school of higher education in Lāʻie. "We believe," he concluded, "that all of this is but the purpose of the Lord unfolding before our eyes."[19]

In President McKay's moving dedicatory prayer, he spoke of the responsibility resting on all Church members "to carry the message of the restoration of the gospel to all nations . . . to present the principles of the gospel in an intelligent manner that the honest in heart may be convinced of the truth, and may be led from paths of error into the way of righteousness." He prayed that those who looked at the college buildings would be influenced to look in turn to God and to contribute their efforts for the blessings of mankind.[20]

In February 1961, just five years after it opened, university accreditation was obtained, making the Church College of Hawaiʻi a four-year institution. Announcement was made some years later, in June 1974, that the CCH was being renamed and would henceforth be called Brigham Young University–Hawaiʻi (BYU–H). The school would retain its full individuality, although its Church-guided dress and health codes, its programs, and its curricula would be those of BYU–Provo. The Church College of Hawaiʻi was "no ordinary college," Dr. Law had said, but a "great institution, conceived in prophetic vision, with a great heritage . . . and [an] important destiny to fulfill."[21]

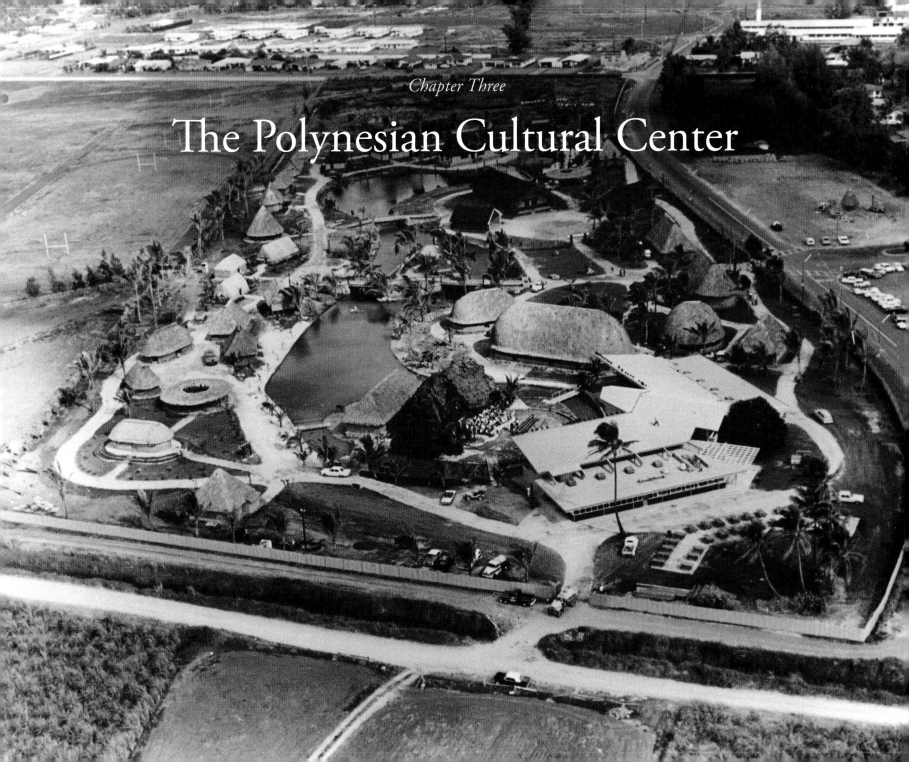

Chapter Three

The Polynesian Cultural Center

POLYNESIAN CULTURAL CENTE

Front entry to the PCC.

By 1960, most of the CCH labor missionaries had dispersed. It seemed that the Labor Missionary Program in Hawai`i was at an end and that David O. McKay's vision of a school had been fulfilled. But already things were happening that would change that. Developments in Lā`ie were not finished, and there was one last piece to be put in place.

Dr. Law had expressed disappointment in 1955 that the CCH opened with the low enrollment of only 153 students. But the following year numbers rose to 291, and by the end of the academic year 1957–58 the student body population had shot up to 402 students. Polynesian students were eager to attend the CCH and were willing to work for their education, but there was one obstacle. Airfare to Hawai`i alone cost hundreds of dollars, a fortune to most Pacific Islanders. Tuition and other expenses also needed to be met, and there were few opportunities to earn this money. In his report at the 1956 commencement exercises, Dr. Law noted that the college had employed seventy-seven students in part-time work (almost half the student body) and given $2,349.60 in grants and scholarships. He added, "May I emphasize that one of our great needs . . . is for part-time job opportunities near[by] . . . so [students] may work part-time while attending school."[1]

The answer to this dilemma revealed itself by addressing another problem. In 1919, when the Lā`ie Temple was dedicated, it was the only one in the Pacific for almost forty years until the New Zealand Temple was dedicated in 1958. It would be twenty-five more years before temples were dedicated in 1983 in Sāmoa, Tonga, and Tahiti. Yet the Church continued to thrive in the islands, and members had a deep longing to receive their ordinances in a temple. They were encouraged by their leaders to do their genealogy and save money to attend the temple in Hawai`i, despite the enormous sacrifices involved in doing so. In some instances, people sold all their possessions, even their homes and clothing, to raise necessary funds for the long trip to Hawai`i.

Matthew Cowley

As a seventeen-year-old young man in 1914,[2] Matthew Cowley was called as a missionary to New Zealand. There he spent five years learning the language, living with the native Māori, and loving the people. In 1938, Cowley was called back to New Zealand as a mission president, and the Māori called him *tumuaki* (president) for another eight years. On October 5, 1945, forty-eight-year-old Cowley sat in the Salt Lake Tabernacle anticipating the beginning of general conference and contemplating his future. He expected to settle down after thirteen years of missionary service and pick up the ends of a promising law career. But at that conference Matthew Cowley found himself being called to the Council of the Twelve by President George Albert Smith, who had

Apostle Matthew Cowley (standing),
Wendell B. Mendenhall, and
Edward L. Clissold.

himself been sustained President of the Church at the very same conference.

Just a year later, in December 1946, the First Presidency created a new position, President of the Pacific Missions of the Church, and assigned Elder Cowley to this post. In fulfilling his new assignment, Elder Cowley assumed full charge of all the missions in the Pacific, including those in Asia. People called him unofficially the "Apostle of the Pacific." For the next three years he traveled almost constantly by air around this vast area to carry out his responsibilities. The announced purposes of his assignment were threefold: first, assess the effects of World War II upon the work of the Church in the islands (the war ended in 1945); second, investigate ways to help Polynesians gather their genealogies and attend the Lā`ie Temple; and third, "study the advisability of establishing Church schools in the Pacific" to improve the education of members there.[3]

Elder Cowley's pursuit of these goals led him to counsel with other Church leaders to find workable solutions, especially with Edward Clissold, a longtime friend and counselor in the Oahu Stake Presidency (he would become president of the Oahu Stake in 1951), and with Wendell B. Mendenhall, one of Cowley's former New Zealand missionaries. Whenever Cowley was with either of them, the conversations continued about what could be done to ease the lack of accommodations in Lā`ie for temple attendees.

Cowley expressed great concern for the Māori who came from New Zealand to attend the Lā`ie Temple. After making all the sacrifices to get to Hawai`i, he said, they had difficulty finding affordable housing in Lā`ie when they arrived (there was no hotel). If a *whare* (house) existed in Lā`ie, it might solve the problem. Cowley further envisioned that the Māori could support themselves by singing and dancing to provide entertainment for tourists. In

1951, after going over the problem again, Clissold responded, "Well, if that's true of the Māori people, it could also be true of the other people who come up. Each one of the island groups could have a place where they could live and display their particular kind of craft or entertainment."[4]

Speaking at the Oahu Stake conference in the Honolulu Tabernacle on March 11, 1951, Elder Cowley said, "I can envision a time when there will be [Polynesian] villages at Lā`ie. They'll have a carved house . . . for the Māoris, . . . a Samoan village, a Tahitian village, and villages for other peoples of the South Seas."[5] It was the first expression from the pulpit of the idea that had been simmering for so long. But many people had heard it expressed privately before. Millie Rogers Tengaio remembered that when she was a young woman, Matthew Cowley visited her home in New Zealand and said, "I'd like to see a Māori carved meeting house built in America."[6] Everyone laughed because it seemed preposterous at the time that Americans would want a carved house there. Hawai`i wasn't even a state. Many years later Millie and her husband, Joseph, would come to Hawai`i as labor missionaries to help build the Māori village at the PCC.

Later, in March 1951, Elder Cowley met with Wendell Mendenhall and discussed the plan with him, and in the summer of 1953 Mendenhall, Clissold, and Cowley met at a reunion in Utah and again discussed island villages in Lā`ie. At each meeting the scope of their plans expanded, and the vision they shared became more specific.

Unfortunately, Elder Matthew Cowley died suddenly in his sleep in 1953 at the age of fifty-six and did not live to see either the Church College of Hawai`i or the Polynesian Cultural Center in reality. But his early vision and work to help the Polynesians remain a large part of their history.

The Pacific Board of Education

On July 29, 1957, President McKay created the Pacific Board of Education to supervise all the schools in the South Pacific, including the Church College of Hawai`i. Wendell Mendenhall was made chairman and Edward Clissold vice chairman. This was a remarkable event, since several years before, in July 1953, the First Presidency had announced the unification of the entire Church system of educational institutions under one head, Dr. Ernest L. Wilkinson. The Pacific Board of Education was the only educational entity in the Church that now operated outside the unified Church school system. The Pacific Board reported directly to the First Presidency, evidence that President McKay maintained a strong desire to personally guide the destiny of the people of the Pacific Islands. Now, as key board members of the Pacific Board of Education, Mendenhall and Clissold traveled together extensively and had much opportunity to talk about the future in Lā`ie.

The Hukilau

Just over 100,000 tourists came to Hawai`i in 1955 when the CCH opened, most of them from the US mainland. The North Shore of Oahu was not a must-see part of the island. The admired Lā`ie Temple was a place to stretch legs and snap a few pictures for island-circling tourists. Lā`ie itself was still a quiet country town with a population of only 1,350 people. The huge tourist industry of Hawai`i—which in 2011 attracted more than seven million visitors and accounted for a whopping one-third of all jobs in Hawai`i—was just getting a head of steam. For sixty-five years a

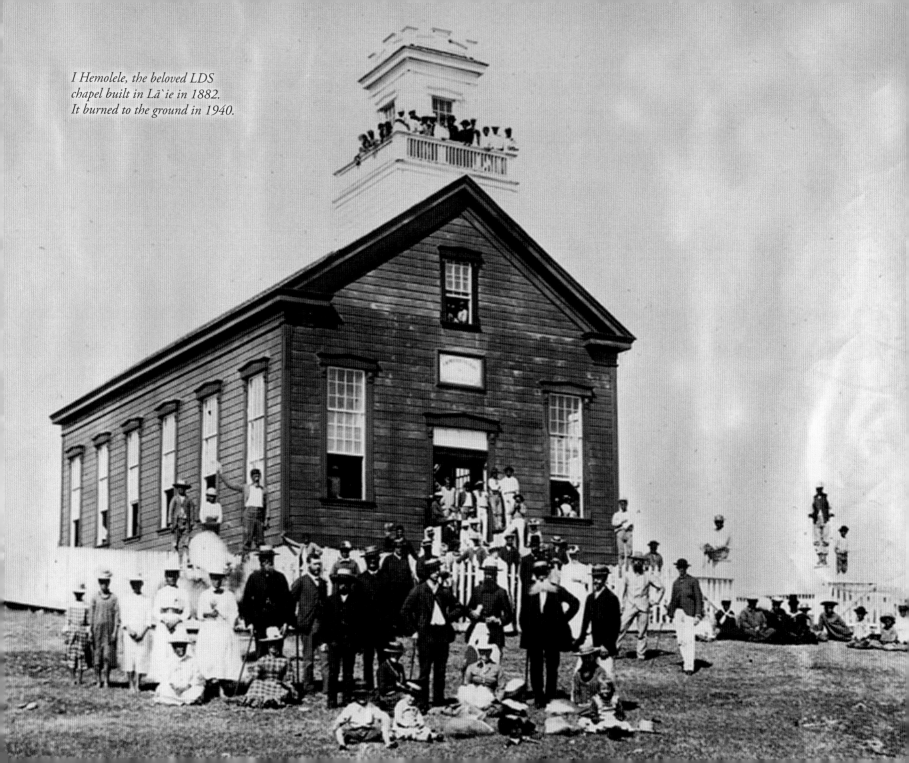

I Hemolele, the beloved LDS chapel built in Lā`ie in 1882. It burned to the ground in 1940.

beloved chapel called *I Hemolele,* meaning holy place, had stood in Lā`ie. In 1882, King Kalakaua and Queen Kapiolani had participated in laying its cornerstone. The king attended the dedication in 1883, and the queen contributed one hundred dollars to the building fund. In 1915, I Hemolele was moved from its choice hilltop site to an adjacent lot to make way for the Lā`ie Temple. By 1940, the aging wooden structure was in need of a coat of paint. In those days, old paint was commonly removed with a blow torch, but in the case of *I Hemolele,* this proved disastrous and the building quickly caught fire.

When the firemen arrived from the nearest station some forty-five miles away, the building was already in ashes. The people tried unsuccessfully to remove pews and other items from the burning structure but they could only stand by helplessly and weep unashamedly. Almost immediately they began planning ways to raise money for a new chapel. However, when Pearl Harbor was bombed in 1941, sweeping the United States into World War II, all new projects ground to a halt and the community of Lā`ie held Sunday worship services in the social hall for the next nine years.

After the war, in 1947, a committee headed by Bishop Po`i Kekauoha began to raise money in earnest for a new chapel. Viola Kawahigashi, a leader in the ward, suggested they hold a *hukilau* (community Hawaiian fishing with nets). The hukilau was not a new idea. Before the war, the Hawai`i Tourist Bureau at Kailua Park on Oahu had paid fishermen to demonstrate hukilau for tourists. Hukilau had even been staged by Church members a few times in the late 1930s to raise funds for the Honolulu Tabernacle, which was dedicated in 1941, just months before Pearl Harbor was bombed. So now, with the support of Lā`ie families, the hukilau was revived. It was initially planned to be held once a month during the winter and twice monthly in the summer.

The idea of the hukilau was that guests would pay to spend a day on the beach fishing with nets, feasting, and being entertained Polynesian style. Enthusiastic tourists heard about the hukilau and attended in increasing numbers. Other groups on Oahu tried to duplicate the Lā`ie hukilau, but none was successful. Lā`ie seemed to have just the right combination of talent, enthusiasm, and *aloha* (love, greeting) spirit to make it all work.

Huki in Hawaiian means "pull," and *lau* means "leaf," so *hukilau* literally means to "pull the leaf." Hawaiian fishing nets were sometimes a quarter of a mile in length and had lau tied to the netting to drive the fish toward shore. Men in outrigger canoes shouted and beat the surface of the water with paddles, further driving the fish and adding to the festive nature of the event. When the ends of the net arrived at the shore, everyone joined in to huki the heavy catch onto the beach. The Hawaiian and Samoan men added to the excitement by popping live fish into their mouths while the tails flapped wildly. They didn't actually eat the fish, but the tourists loved it.

The net pulling was a big draw by itself, but then a luau and entertainment were added to the hukilau, and these elements became a major part of its success. For three dollars, tourists could buy a whole day's activity. They were greeted on the beach with lei (flower garlands) and music, and the net pulling occupied the morning. The festivities were climaxed by a midday luau, which included two or three whole pigs baked in the *imu* (underground oven). Guests sat on mats Polynesian style and enjoyed a feast of *poi* (a traditional food made from taro), *lomilomi salmon,* *kālua* (steamed pork), chicken, baked fresh fish, heaping bowls of fresh fruit, and *haupia* (coconut pudding). After the luau, the Hawaiians and Samoans involved the whole crowd in a Polynesian song and dance fest. Most Lā`ie residents, from preschool children

The Ali'i, representing Hawaiian royalty, welcome visitors to the hukilau.

Uncovering the imu.

Christmas at the hukilau.

Aerial view of the infrastructure on Hukilau Beach.

Hukilau fishermen tease guests by popping wriggling fish into their mouths.

The Waikiki
BEACH PRESS

HAWAII'S LARGEST VISITOR CIRCULATION

Vol. XIII, No. 57   WAIKIKI, HAWAIIAN ISLANDS   July 17-20, 1967

Fish, Feast And Frolic At Laie Hukilau

Haul Net, Eat A Lot At Hukilau

It's hukilau time in Hawaii and the fishing festival staged at Laie Bay is a visitor must.

Circle Saturday, July 22, from 9:30 a.m. to 2 p.m. on your calendar for the next hukilau.

The event is presented twice monthly during the summer.

Tickets sell at $5 and may be obtained at the Hawaii Visitors Bureau, phone 931-181. Transportation may be arranged through tour offices.

The schedule of events during the day is as follows:

9:30 to 10 a.m., browsing around old Laie Bay; 10 to 10:30 a.m., Hawaiian family activities; 10:30 to 10:45 a.m., uncovering of the imu (earth oven).

10:45 to 11 a.m., view Polynesian games; 11 to 11:30 a.m., Samoan family activities; 11:30 to noon, hukilau or Hawaiian community fishing.

Noon to 1 p.m., luau or feasting of Hawaiian food, 1 to 2 p.m., hour of Polynesian entertainment featuring Samoans, Hawaiians, Maoris, Tahitians and Tongans.

The fishing, feasting and traditional dances and songs of Polynesia will be brilliantly presented to the visitor at this time, a special bonanza for camera fans.

Originally a community fishing festival in which the catch was shared by participants, the hukilau has been expanded into a prime visitor attraction by Hawaiian and Samoan inhabitants of the village of Laie.

Part of the fun is in getting to Laie. The drive from Waikiki, over Nuuanu Pali with its world-renowned view, along Windward Oahu's beaches and coastal communities, takes about one hour.

Villagers have long since been at work preparing food for the luau.

Many lean luau pigs are stuffed with hot lava rocks and placed in a huge underground oven called an imu. Island breadfruit, laulaus and sweet potatoes are steamed with the pork.

While waiting for the feast to be served, guests may witness exhibitions of other native skills.

'EVERYBODY LOVES A HUKILAU'—A riot of color explodes at the exciting hukilau (fishing festival) at picturesque old Laie Bay made famous in song and dance. Bright Island aloha shirts, muumuus and brilliant tropical flowers add to the gaiety of the community-styled feast. The traditional Laie hukilau is more than 20 years old. Next one is scheduled on Saturday, July 22, from 9:30 a.m. to 2 p.m., and visitors may see the nets being thrown into the sea "and the amaama come swimming in." It's a scenic drive from Waikiki to Laie, near the northern point of Oahu Island. There'll be fun fishing, feasting at a luau and watching a colorful Polynesian program of native dancing and singing.

—John Bonsey Photo Courtesy Laie Hukilau

Five Luaus Cater To The Malihini

Right in the heart of Waikiki five colorful and authentic luaus with sparkling Polynesian entertainment are offered weekly.

Hilton Hawaiian Village holds luaus on Wednesday and Sunday beginning with cocktails at 6 p.m. The charge is $9 per person and reservations may be made by calling 994-321.

The Queen's Surf luaus are staged Thursday and Sunday at 6:30 p.m. Reservations for the $9 feast should be phoned in to 937-387.

The Sunday Royal Hawaiian Hotel luau costs $10 and begins at 6:30 p.m. Call the hotel at 937-311 for reservations.

All of these luaus cater to the newcomer, who may wear informal Hawaiian clothes -- aloha shirts for the men and muumuus, holokus and full-skirted sun dresses for the women.

History Of Fashions At Luncheon-Pageant

Depicting the development of costumes, songs and dances of Hawaii from ancient times through the monarchy to the present, "Memories of Old Hawaii" will be produced August 3 and 8.

Hilton Hawaiian Village Dome will be the setting for the colorful fund-raising event of the Daughters of Hawaii.

Hawaiian music will be heard during no-host cocktail time, beginning at 11:30 a.m. Luncheon will be served at 12:30 p.m.

The pageant, planned by Miss Winona Love and Mrs. Herbert K. Keppeler, will begin at 1:15 p.m. It will be staged and directed by Maiki Aiu and the Hula Halau o Maiki.

The Hawaii Chapter of the American Bar Association asked the Daughters of Hawaii to sponsor a show and luncheon for visiting members.

Due to the capacity of the
(Continued on Page 16)

to grandparents, played instruments (either the ukulele, steel guitar, or string bass), and danced or sang in the show, which included *kahiko* (ancient-style *hula*), `auana (modern-style *hula*), and chants. Hundreds of Lā`ie children learned to dance so they could participate.[7] The fireknife dance was even performed at the hukilau on special occasions by Siliwa Anae Kaleikini. A narrator introduced and explained each number to the audience. The Lā`ie hukilau became the inspiration for the song "We're Going to the Hukilau," composed by Jack Owens in 1948, which became widely popular.

To better accommodate the hukilau, an infrastructure began to grow on Hukilau Beach, which was enlarged and improved over the years. A dilapidated army mess hall was moved to the beach to serve as a dining room. A stage area, outdoors on the sand, was constructed with wooden planks, the crashing ocean waves as a backdrop. Eventually bleachers were borrowed from nearby Kahuku High School to seat as many as fifteen hundred people for the afternoon entertainment. In its final form, there was a stage, the dining hall (with the termite-eaten walls always attractively hidden by flowers), concession buildings to demonstrate and sell handmade crafts, the imu for roasting pigs, and Hawaiian and Samoan huts—all built by the families of Lā`ie. In the early 1960s, the labor missionaries building the Polynesian Cultural Center (PCC) added masonry bleachers, a rock-bordered stage, and new restrooms to the complex.

Visiting Church authorities also enjoyed the hukilau. When Apostle Spencer W. Kimball visited Lā`ie in 1946 while on a four-week tour of the islands, he enthusiastically waded into the ocean up to his chest to help pull in the heavy, fish-laden nets, to the delight of the local members. He was told later that most Church leaders who attended usually just watched from the beach.[8]

In its first three years the hukilau raised over $40,000 toward construction of the new chapel in Lā`ie, which was dedicated by Elder Matthew Cowley on April 1, 1950. But after meeting that goal, the hukilau continued until the early 1970s and ran concurrent with the operation of the PCC for several years, averaging about eight hundred guests a month. Besides the financial benefit, the hukilau proved two critical things to doubters. Given enough incentive, tourists would drive from Waikiki to visit Lā`ie, and they would pay to enjoy authentic Polynesian food, music, and dance.

Today all the old structures have long been removed from Hukilau Beach, but many of the elements of the hukilau are preserved at the Polynesian Cultural Center down the road. Besides being successful in its own right, the hukilau was a prototype for the PCC. It proved it could be done and that obstacles could be overcome, thus blazing the trail to accomplish it all.

Bringing in the catch at the hukilau.

Hukilau

THE ENCHANTING STORY OF LAIE'S

CELEBRATED HUKILAU TRADITION

Folklore has it that another Hawaiian tradition grew out of the Lāʻie hukilau: the now world-popular shaka hand wave. Hamana Kalili, whose boat house was on Hukilau Beach and who often provided boats and nets for the hukilau, had lost the three middle fingers of his right hand in an accident. When Kalili waved at visitors with his damaged hand, people began waving back, imitating his action by curling up their three middle fingers and only extending their thumb and little finger. The wave gained popularity quickly, and the shaka was born. Locals added the "hang loose" greeting, and the wave became familiar throughout the islands and beyond.

Hamana Kalili poses as Hawaiian royalty to promote the hukilau.

POLYNESIAN
PANORAMA
(Authentic Polynesian Dances)

**MAORI • SAMOAN
HAWAIIAN • TONGAN**

Presented By
The Polynesian Institute of
The Church College of Hawaii
at the

KAISER DOME

April 14th & 15th
Fri. & Sat. 8 P.M.

PRICES:
Reserved $2.50
General
    Admission....$2.00
Children
    under 12 ......$1.50

**ORDER YOUR
TICKETS NOW!**

Advertisement for the Polynesian Panorama.

Polynesian Panorama

Edward Clissold, as chairman of the board of the CCH, has been given credit for suggesting that students could be trained to perform authentic Polynesian entertainment that tourists would pay to watch. Richard Wootton, second president of the CCH, and two talented members of his faculty, Jerry Loveland and Wiley Swapp, discussed it, and the idea was enthusiastically accepted. This time the hukilau dancers would be the trainers, and the CCH students would be the performers. Intensive instruction began under Ruihi Hemmingsen of New Zealand, who instructed the students in Māori dance and song. Hawaiian Christine Nauahi and Samoan Chief Galea`i Tuia Feagaimaali`i, who had both been working with dancers in the hukilau, became involved, and Wiley Swapp was put in charge.

Student performances were worked into the hukilau program for practice and experience. The first professional performance of the seventy-five-member group was in April 1960. To give confidence to the students they had helped train, members of the hukilau entertainers joined the students on stage. They filled the Kaiser Dome at the Hilton Hawaiian Village Hotel on Waikiki on successive nights for a program called *Polynesian Panorama*. The students spent five hours travel time and earned just five dollars each. If they were to support themselves through their singing and dancing, this was not an auspicious beginning. But it was obvious from the enthusiastic reception of the audiences—used to the more staid performances of Waikiki professionals—that the students were exciting and refreshing and definitely a hit, another confirmation that tourists would pay to watch such entertainment.

Many Polynesian students lacked knowledge of their own native cultures and had to be taught songs and dances from the ground up, revealing the necessity of researching and collecting a library of films, tapes, books, and information to preserve the authentic dances, chants, songs, and cultures of Polynesia, and creating a repository to hold this information. For this purpose the Polynesian Institute was organized as an adjunct of the Church College of Hawai`i, with Jerry Loveland as director. A class called *Halau `Imi No`eau* (school seeking wisdom and skill) was offered at the CCH, the name suggested by Mary Kawena Puku`i. Since then many groups have followed suit and organized their own halau. The term is common in Hawai`i today (and elsewhere where hula is taught) and usually refers to a hula school or troupe. With the organization of the Polynesian Institute, the preservation of authentic Polynesian culture became an important objective of the CCH and strengthened the idea of creating villages in Lā`ie where authentic entertainment could be performed for tourists. The Polynesian Institute, now called the Jonathan Napela Center for Hawaiian and Pacific Island Studies at Brigham Young University–Hawai`i, continues its mission today to preserve and document Polynesian culture and history.

Polynesian Panorama *dancers prepare for their performance.*

The Polynesian Cultural Center

The dream of Church leaders, starting with Elder Matthew Cowley and carried on by Clissold and Mendenhall, who all loved Polynesia and who could envision villages representing various island groups, eventually bore fruit. The commercial success of the hukilau, the enthusiastic reception of *Polynesian Panorama* and other small entertainments, the desire to preserve authentic Polynesian culture, and the growing financial needs of the CCH students all came together in 1961 with the decision by the Church to build Polynesian villages in Lāʻie. It was a practical solution for many needs.

Many names were considered and rejected for the enterprise until Wiley Swapp suggested the "Polynesian Cultural Center." Edward Clissold liked it immediately. They presented it to the First Presidency, and it was officially accepted.

On February 12, 1961 (exactly six years to the day after the groundbreaking for the CCH), the First Presidency approved a $15,000 appropriation to cover the immediate costs of planning the new center. Douglas Burton, who had helped design the CCH's permanent campus and whose father many years before had designed the Lāʻie Temple, was appointed to draw up the plans. He immediately embarked on a two-year tour of Polynesia to study native building techniques so his drawings would be as accurate as possible.

President McKay asked Edward Clissold to send a working paper summarizing the purposes of the Center, which he did on August 10, 1961. Clissold listed the purposes as follows: 1) "To preserve through research and expert guidance the entertainment arts and the crafts of the several Polynesian races"; 2) "To exploit in a dignified manner the tourist's desire to see the Polynesian entertainment and . . . [earn] possible revenue"; and 3) To provide employment opportunities for Lāʻie residents and "part-time work for students at the College."[9]

CHOOSING A SITE

Now a building site in Lāʻie had to be identified. The obvious choice was Hukilau Beach, where tourists already came to attend the hukilau and where existing structures might be utilized. In fact, a sketch was made by a Honolulu architect showing the addition of several buildings on the beach, the first visualization of a Polynesian center. But the site had serious problems. One major issue was that the narrow area proposed was squeezed between the highway and the ocean, leaving little room for development and no room for parking, forcing visitors to cross the highway on foot from a parking lot. Another drawback was that the windy weather on the beach made it difficult to develop landscaping. Also, it was too far away from the temple. Planners hoped that the temple parking lot could be shared by the PCC.

The field between the temple and the college (where faculty and student housing is currently located) was selected as the new location, and work began. Fill was added to strengthen the soil, the area was fenced, and a lagoon was partially excavated. But concerns were raised about this site too, mainly because of its proximity to the temple, and the worry that noise created by the Center would be at variance with the sacred nature of the temple experience.

In November 1961, construction was temporarily halted, and President McKay sent Elders Delbert L. Stapley and Gordon B. Hinckley of the Quorum of the Twelve to thoroughly investigate the

Wiley Swapp helped organize student entertainers from the CCH to demonstrate their native dances at the International Marketplace in Waikiki.

Polynesian structures begin to rise around a newly constructed lagoon on the PCC site in 1962.

entire undertaking. They held many long meetings, toured the site, and concluded that construction should be deferred until they could report their findings in Salt Lake City. President McKay approved a change of venue for the Center to a twelve-acre *lo`i kalo* (taro patch) adjacent to the CCH campus on Kamehameha Highway.

With the site determined, construction moved forward. The plan called for the creation of six Polynesian villages, which corresponded coincidentally to the islands visited by President McKay on his 1921 world tour—Hawai`i, New Zealand, Fiji, Tahiti, Tonga, and Sāmoa. A freshwater lagoon would snake among the villages, giving them each water access.

OFFICIAL INCORPORATION

On August 14, 1963, Wendell Mendenhall and Edward Clissold were instructed to formally organize the Polynesian Cultural Center as a Hawaiian nonprofit corporation, directly responsible to the Pacific Board of Education of the LDS Church. Everyone was cautiously optimistic that it could be successful, but there was only a slight glimmer of what this venture would eventually become.

On August 28, 1963, Howard B. Stone became the first general manager of the Center, with six assistant managers, one for each village. A board of directors was appointed with Wendell B. Mendenhall as chairman and Edward Clissold as vice chairman. All of the members of the Pacific Board of Education were made board members, and the president of the CCH, dean of students, and the director of the Polynesian Institute were named ex officio board members. Six weeks later, on October 14, 1963, the Center opened for business.

The board of directors has been a great strength to the PCC over the years. To date, sixty-eight extremely capable men and women have served as members. Some have had business backgrounds and were CEOs and officers of a wide variety of well-known national companies. There have been entrepreneurs who built their own companies, highly placed academics, a judge, and a Tongan woman who danced in the first PCC night show. Some have been Polynesians and some haole, all experienced and capable. This group, serving without compensation, has made enormous contributions in shaping the policies of the PCC and appointing its officers.

For thirty-one years, both the chairman and vice-chairman of the board were members of the Quorum of the Twelve Apostles. Elder Howard W. Hunter served as chairman of the board from 1965 until 1976 (he was president of the Church from 1994 to 1995). Elder Marvin J. Ashton was chairman from 1976 to 1988, when Elder Dallin H. Oaks replaced him, with Joseph B. Wirthlin as vice-chairman. In 1996, General Authorities were released from all such callings because of the great increase in their ecclesiastical responsibilities. The representation of members of the Twelve on the PCC board shows the essential support of the Church that the Center has enjoyed over the years. It has benefited immeasurably from such wise and steady leadership.

Even today, after almost fifty years, the PCC's name and mission have not changed. It is still a nonprofit Hawaiian corporation. No chairman or director has ever received a penny for services. The Center does charge admission to help cover operational expenses, but excess revenues, according to its charter, stay in Lā`ie and go to the Center for improvements or to BYU–Hawai`i either as grants, scholarships, or as remuneration for services given by the student employees.

LABOR MISSIONARY PROGRAM REVIVED

To build the Center, the Labor Missionary Program was revived after a five-year hiatus. Recruiting the missionaries proved to be yet again one of the most memorable episodes in the history

Local volunteers who helped build the PCC.

of the Church's building program. In his continuing capacity as chairman of the Labor Missionary Program, Wendell Mendenhall went to Tonga first, where the mission president called a meeting of former labor missionaries. Mendenhall immediately got down to business. "I asked the brethren how many were married," he recalled. "Thirteen of them raised their hands, [but] one of the hands went down very quickly. I said how many of [you] married men are willing to leave [your] wife for two or two and a half years? Every hand came up. The hand of the youngest of the married men came up and went down very quickly, and he said: 'President Mendenhall, I just got married today. Will you give me a chance to tell my wife?'"[10] All thirty-one accepted a mission call to Hawai`i. Next, Mendenhall went to Sāmoa. Twenty-four former labor missionaries declared they were also ready to go to Hawai`i.

Tongan labor missionaries in 1962.

In New Zealand, Mendenhall met with eighteen men who had helped build the CCH campus. A spokesman answered for all of them, saying, "We are here. We are here to go to work on this project. We will finish this job and want you to know that we are ready to go to any other place in the world you would like to send us."[11] All eighteen came to Hawai`i.

Meanwhile, Clissold contacted US immigration officials in Hawai`i, alerting them to the plans to bring Polynesians into the country. He applied for their admission on the grounds that their special knowledge of their own cultures and handicrafts was essential to building the Polynesian villages, that they would be given job training in construction work, and that they would be taking classes at the Church College of Hawai`i and therefore qualify as students. They were given permission to enter the United States.

The Tongans went by steamship to Pago Pago, American Sāmoa, where they joined the Samoans, and all fifty-five boarded a Pan American flight to Honolulu. Flight attendants said the missionaries sang songs all the way across the ocean to the delight of passengers and crew, and everyone hated to see the flight end. Arriving in Honolulu, they boarded a bus for the trip to Lā`ie. Now all was in place to make the dream of a cultural center a reality. By the time the project ended, 165 Polynesians and 139 members from the US mainland, for a total of 305, had joined the great labor force.

One of the great privileges that the Tongan and Samoan building missionaries had looked forward to in Hawai`i was attending the Lā`ie Temple for their own ordinances. This became a reality soon after they arrived when on May 3, 1960, forty-seven of them went to the temple together. At the time this was the largest number of endowments for the living ever done in the Lā`ie Temple in one session. 🌿

Chapter Four

Gathered in a Lo`i Kalo

Excavating rocks for the PCC by hand.

The second Hawaiian labor missionary project began in January 1960 and lasted almost until the end of 1963. It consisted of four different large construction projects, and constructing the Polynesian Cultural Center was not only one item on a long agenda, it was the last to get started. At the CCH, new student dormitories, faculty housing, and six other projects were built. At the Lā`ie Temple, missionaries replaced the old Bureau of Information with a new visitors' center, and installed extensive landscaping, among other things.

Fourteen new or renovated LDS chapels in Hawai`i—including seven on Oahu, five on the island of Hawai`i, and one each on Maui and Moloka`i—were finished. The project expanded into Asia, where four chapels were constructed—two in Japan, and one each in Korea and Taiwan.

After two years the missionaries were finally ready to start building the Polynesian Cultural Center. There was no formal groundbreaking. One day in early February 1962, heavy equipment was moved onto the taro patch and digging began. As with the CCH construction, the ground was soft and spongy and had to be strengthened with two feet of crushed coral to support the roads and villages of the Center.

The next item on the agenda was to dig the lagoon, but none of the labor missionaries had ever constructed a lagoon before. One had been started at the original PCC site, but it only amounted to a hole in the ground, now abandoned and filled in. The plan was to stake the lagoon and dig out the basin with heavy machinery. Then wooden forms could be installed around the perimeter for the walls. Hawaiian labor missionary Bill Kanahele saw a better way. He suggested digging a five-foot-deep trench around

the perimeter of the lagoon first, wide enough to accommodate the steel and concrete for the walls, which would be installed right behind the trench digger. The dirt walls of the trench would serve as forms for the concrete, eliminating the need to buy wood and construct forms, saving both time and money. After the concrete hardened, equipment could be moved inside the lagoon area to excavate the water basin. Kanahehe was convincing, and his plan worked just as he had foreseen. When the inside of the lagoon was finally dug, "[It was] beautiful," says Kanahehe. "[We] didn't have to do [anything else] to the walls."[1]

To support all of this construction, a block house, mechanic shop, sheet metal shop, and carpentry mill were soon functioning behind the PCC site. All of the concrete blocks used in the projects were made on-site. In addition, the hills directly behind the project provided the coral and volcanic rock that was used as fill in the concrete, the various rock walls, and the other building elements, as well as in the ground to strengthen it.

Heavy equipment was necessary to remove some of the massive stones, which weighed several thousand pounds and were used to form the mountain background for the stage in the new theater and in other places. Workers struggled with digging bars and fork-lifts to dislodge boulders and then secured them with heavy cables to be hoisted by crane onto trucks, which could often carry only a single boulder because of its size and weight. Smaller stones were floated down the lagoon on rafts.

The labor missionaries worked from drawings prepared by architect Douglas Burton, who had researched Polynesian construction styles and techniques, but the final factor of success was the native men and women who not only did the manual work, but who also brought expert knowledge of building techniques and total commitment from their islands, and used it all to bring a high level of authenticity to each of the villages. Without these dedicated Saints, the Center could never have been completed.

Building the Villages

Every effort was made to use strictly native materials in the PCC village structures. Most of the perimeter posts or columns and structural logs in the native houses were of `ohi`a wood shipped from the island of Hawai`i. These were stripped of their bark on-site by hand. Some coconut logs were used and prepared in the same way. The intricate framework of the buildings cannot be seen as clearly from the outside of the houses as they are covered with bamboo, fern, thatch, or reeds, but is readily discernible from the interior of the buildings.

SENNIT

With no metal available in Polynesia, building techniques used `afa` (sennit) lashings to tie everything together. Sennit is the most common string and rope of Polynesia. Made from coconut husks, the strands are first soaked and beaten to remove fibrous filler. Then, to obtain lengths of uniform thickness, several fibers are rolled together between the hands or against the thigh. Last, the strands are braided into cords of desired length and strength. The practical need for sennit in the islands was so constant that its fabrication was a continuous enterprise. Observers note that because of its usefulness, sennit was the most important single article manufactured in Polynesia. Large coils of it were kept on hand for household use and as an article of exchange.

Most of the sennit for the Center was shipped from Sāmoa and Tonga, but some was made on-site. Luse Tapusoa Magalei remembers as a child the gatherings to weave and make sennit. The women did the weaving and also prepared the `afa, or coconut husk fibers. Then the men sat cross-legged under a shade tree, pulled up their *lavalava* (men's wrapped skirt), rolled the sennit on their thighs and braided it into strands miles and miles long. People laughed, told stories, joked, and sang songs. They'd bring lunch and work most of the day. The children were kept busy running errands back and forth or preparing lunch in the `umu for their elders. Magalei said it was work, but it didn't seem like work.

To hold the framework of the buildings together, a variety of intricate lashings was employed both for strength and decoration. The lashings in the Center were done by native master artisans and are beautiful works of art in and of themselves. Matagi Uga Alo did most of the lashing in the Samoan buildings, Isireli Racule in the Fijian village, and Semisi `Olive and Nafetalai Alusa in the Tongan *fale* (houses). Thousands of yards of sennit were required to build the Samoan Village alone, according to Vaimanino Tofa. To watch these masters lash the sennit was mesmerizing. For variety and beauty, some of the sennit was dyed various colors using a swamp plant, adding to the artistry of the lashings.

TOP LEFT AND BOTTOM RIGHT: *Intricate lashings used to hold the buildings together.*
TOP RIGHT AND BOTTOM CENTER: *Pole framings were used in all the Polynesian buildings.*
BOTTOM LEFT: *Braiding `afa or sennit.*

Each island group also has its own distinctive style of thatching that covers the roofs and walls of the Polynesian structures. At the PCC, every attempt was made to use the correct materials, and where that was not possible, sugarcane lau, then readily available in Hawai`i, was used to finish and thatch the buildings.

Harvesting the sugarcane lau for thatch was a major effort. CCH students working without pay, Lā`ie townspeople of all ages, and many volunteers went to the Center each day under the direction of James Uale to help decorate, landscape, and complete the villages. They were involved especially in collecting the lau, an uncomfortable and bothersome job. Auntie Fuatino Kouhou remembered that they'd catch the truck to Haleiwa while it was still dark to pick the sugarcane leaves. They'd wait on the truck until the sun came up and then fill it with lau.

Only dry leaves can be taken from living cane without damaging the plant. Cane lau have sharp edges with tiny needle-like hairs growing everywhere. For protection in the cane fields, the workers had to cover themselves from head to toe, making the work much hotter. They wore knee-length rubber boots while they slogged up and down the rows of cane. When they had enough lau for a bundle, they'd tie it together and stack it beside the road to be loaded onto a truck and hauled to Lā`ie. On rainy days their feet would sink into the mud in the fields, sometimes up to their thighs. Then they'd have to call someone to pull the older people out and carry them out of the field. Back at the Center, the lau still had to be woven before it could be applied onto the houses.

Sugarcane lau was not used for thatching the Fijian buildings or the Hawaiian *hale* (houses). Traditionally Hawaiians thatched with *pili*, a long coarse grass that is resistant to heavy weather. By the time the PCC was built, though, pili was found increasingly only on private or government land. One source was on the Kohala side of the Big Island, and Bill Sproat was in charge of harvesting it and sending it by barge to Oahu.

The Fijian Village Is Born

The cultural specialist for the Fijian Village was Isireli Racule, a retired schoolteacher with twenty-five years of service, including five as a supervisor of more than one hundred schools. Isireli was intensely interested in preserving his native Fijian culture and had formed a troupe of entertainers who performed for Britain's Queen Elizabeth II when she visited the country. In 1963, he was contacted by Edward Clissold, who was scouting in Fiji for talent to help build the Fijian Village. Isireli gathered fifty of his entertainers to perform for Clissold, who recognized their expertise and invited them to come to Hawai`i to finish the village. They arrived on

The exterior wall of this building shows the patterned thatching on a Fijian hut.

October 7, 1963, just a week before the dedication of the Center and in five days and nights they completed the construction. After tying the last sennit cord, they performed in the opening night show, introducing Fijian dance to Hawai`i.

The original village consisted of a temple, a meetinghouse, a chief's house, and two common houses. Instead of sugarcane daru, the roofs were covered with *balabala* fern, gathered in the mountains behind Lā`ie, under Isireli's direction. Two of the houses were finished with bamboo walls, another with fern, and the last two with grass gathered near Sunset Beach. Due to the unavailability of traditional materials, some adjustments had to be made to the materials used in the buildings. Still, the traditional look has been maintained as much as possible.

One reason Isireli brought so many workers to Hawai`i was to honor Fijian tradition. With the major chiefs in attendance, the village could be blessed in the native way. It was his way of announcing to all Fijians, as well as their ancestors, that they were establishing a Fijian village on a new site, or mat, in the world. In all aspects, the PCC village is an authentic representation of Fiji in the latter part of the nineteenth century.

Construction of the Tahitian Village

Taroaiti Tehani and his wife, Tetua, came to Lā`ie from Pape`ete, Tahiti, to help build the Tahitian Village at the PCC. In Pape`ete, Taroaiti had been a carpenter and farmer and had served in the Church as second counselor in the district presidency. Tetua was born in Pape`ete. Neither spoke English, so Leila Tuhoe, a Tahitian studying at the CCH, acted as interpreter and assistant to the Tehanis.

The newly completed Tahitian Village.

In the original Tahitian Village there were five *fare,* including the *fare bure* (house of god, or temple). The cone-shaped fare bure was strictly authentic in design and was one of the most distinctive structures at the Center, although it no longer stands. It was built on a circular cement foundation. Scaffolding was built in the center of the structure to facilitate construction of the cone-shaped roof and was removed after the rafters and thatching were completed. There were also the *fare ri`i vahine* (queen's house), the *fare taotora`a* (sleeping house), *fare tutu* (kitchen), and the *fare haupape* (which stood on stilts).

In 1973, the Tahitian Village was relocated as part of a major renovation project at the Center. Eventually, four of the five original fare were rebuilt in new locations. The Tahitian Village continued to evolve. Raymond T. Mariteragi (who served as head of the Tahitian Village from 1994 to 2006), was asked to come up with a new design for Tahiti. He spent two years planning the village, including meeting in Tahiti with the minister of culture. The minister wisely concluded that because the Tahitian culture was more familiar to outsiders than were other cultures in French Polynesia, the structures in the village should represent only Tahiti. Other cultures would be represented by a display—wood carvings from the Marquesas, long skirts made from hibiscus from Tahiti, and black pearls from the Tuamotu and Gambier islands. Also on display are skin drums and several elaborate headdresses exquisitely adorned with seashells.

Leila Tuhoe was only one of many Tahitian students who threw their support to the village when they weren't in school. Therese Terooatea Cummings was another who left Tahiti and sixteen siblings in 1961, as a young girl all alone, to enroll at the CCH. Cummings dedicated all her spare time toward building the village.

Carving the Village of Aotearoa into Existence

When Polynesians arrived in Aotearoa, the temperate climate and terrain challenged their traditional survival skills. Of the original plants brought by the colonists, only the *kumara* (sweet potato) thrived. Of necessity, their diet changed to include seafood, fern roots, berries, native birds, and freshwater eels. The cooler weather required warmer clothing made from woven flax and animal skins instead of tapa. Native trees and plants were quickly adopted as building materials for sturdier houses, which is one reason Māori houses and buildings look different from those of other Polynesian cultures. The Māori also became expert woodcarvers. Large *whare nui* (carved buildings) are the focal points of Māori tribal, ancestral, chiefly, and spiritual values. These buildings are the most

symbolic in Polynesia and are considered sacred by the Māori. Each represents a great ancestor who served his people exceptionally well. Some people still live in whare today, and those buildings are also used for *hui* (gatherings) and other purposes. The name of the largest whare at the PCC is *Te Aroha O Te Iwi Māori* (the Great Love of the Māori People). It is the most important building in the village of Aotearoa.

Most of the wood carvings displayed in the PCC Māori Village were carved at Hamilton, New Zealand, and then installed in Lā`ie. In 1947, the Church selected eight young Māori men to work as waged apprentices under two renowned master carvers, brothers Pine and Hone Taiapa. Pine and Hone were already well-known carvers, having largely restored the art among their people. Fourteen years later, these apprentices—Epanaia Whaanga (Barney) Christy, Anaru Kohu, Taka Panere, and Oliphant McKay,

Wood carvers of Aotearoa, including Barney Christy and Arthur Elkington at left.

A carved *tekoteko* (ancestor figure) stands at the gable apex of the whare. A *'koruru* (carved face) on the gable of the meeting house often represents the ancestor after which the house is named. The whole house represents the ancestor's body, with the ridgepole as his backbone. It is a genealogical representation of the ancestry of the tribe, linked together by rafters with *kowhaiwhai* (painted scroll ornamentation), symbolizing the cycles of life from the natural world. The designs are often symbolic of levels of genealogical ties.

now master carvers themselves—were called from the original eight labor missionaries to do the carvings for the PCC. John Arthur Elkington, also a building missionary, was in charge. The carvers worked from drawings that had to be followed precisely so that everything would fit together when it was assembled in Lā`ie.

For two years they toiled on hundreds of pieces. They had a deep sense of mission to represent their Māori culture. "It was a great task," Christy said. "The lumber was donated by a Church member, . . . Taite Davis from North Auckland. Some of these logs were massive and looked impossible to carve. Every day was started with a prayer and a hymn. . . . Many times we worked ten to twelve hours a day. Sometimes in an evening I would look up at the workshop from my lodgings and see the shop lights on. I would walk up to the workshop to find someone carving. Then I would start. And before long, the whole crew would be working. This happened very frequently."[2]

The finished carvings arrived at the PCC only five months before the opening of the Center, to a great welcoming ceremony. But much work still remained. Through the summer months and into the fall, the Māori carvers worked long shifts, twenty-four hours a day, not begrudging anything, to complete their tasks. Every piece had to fit perfectly, and it did. "When I worked on the Māori Village," said Percy TeHira, "it was as though I was representing all the people before me, generations of people. I felt the spirit of my people. I couldn't work long enough. I would finish work late at night or early in the morning just to be around it and to feel the spirit."[3] It was a sacred experience for all.

Viewed together, the carved houses at the PCC are probably the finest collection of Māori carvings found outside of New Zealand. Matthew Cowley would have rejoiced that his vision of a carved house in Lā`ie had been realized.

Building the Village of Hawai`i

In Hawai`i, a family, or `ohana, lived together in a *kauhale*, or collection of buildings—each building having a specific use, such as sleeping, eating, working, arts training, or fishing. This concept was represented by a similar kauhale in the Hawaiian Village, where four houses and two canoe shelters were originally built. The fisherman's house was raised several feet above ground and had a bamboo floor.

The buildings had to conform to building codes, and so other accommodations were made at the Center. Ancient Hawaiian hale didn't have windows, so windows had to be added to the buildings at the PCC for cross ventilation and for the comfort of the many, many people going through the house every day.

All the buildings were covered with Hawaiian pili grass gathered from Maui and the island of Hawai`i. Inside, the ceilings and walls were covered with *lauhala* (leaf of the *hala* tree) woven in

This completed hut in the Hawaiian Village shows fish nets placed over the roof to protect it from the wind.

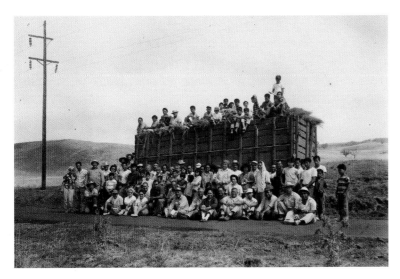

a most striking and interesting manner. A *hikie'e* (woven mattress) furnished one of the houses. The surfaces of a hikie'e, also intricately woven of lauhala, formed a boxlike structure, and the hollow middle was stuffed with waste pieces left from the weaving. The original mattress took three or four women nearly four months of weaving to complete.

Construction of the Samoan Village

The Samoan Village originally consisted of three houses, or *fale*: the guesthouse, the long house, and the *maota tofa,* (the chief's house), all built around a beautiful grassy *marae* (village green), a traditional arrangement in any Samoan village. The marae is the site of special gatherings, ceremonies, and activities. Villagers ensure that the marae is always meticulously landscaped as a showplace of welcome and pride.

Uga Aloa Masasau, a *tufuga* (building specialist) from American Sāmoa, was asked to spearhead the Samoan building project at the Center. Later on, Falefitu Masoe, another well-known tufuga, was engaged in the finish work, along with Pat Peters and Pasi Fuamatu. The perimeter posts of all three fale are of ohi'a wood, as in the rest of the Center, but the large timbers are Douglas fir and the rafters and purlins (the large beams supporting the rafters) are redwood. The large fale is a majestic 102 feet long and 50 feet wide. It took 162 yards of concrete to pour the floor and foundation.

Because of Sāmoa's tropical climate, fale are usually left without walls and are pleasantly light and airy. However, the openings between columns are equipped with woven *polataufafo* (blinds similar to Roman shades) that can be lowered to protect the house during storm or wind. When bamboo was initially put on the fale,

Volunteers went to the big island of Hawai'i to harvest pili grass to thatch the Hawaiian huts. It was sent by barge to Lā'ie.

Mauga Tapusoa, the first chief of the Samoan Village, insisted it be removed, saying that Samoan houses were mainly built of native trees, not bamboo. It was removed.

Student volunteers and Lā`ie townspeople collected small, smooth stones for some of the fale floors to cover the concrete foundations, instead of the gravel mandated by law, making the appearance of the floors much more beautiful. The stones were found in a streambed at Hau`ula near Lā`ie. Thousands of hours of labor were donated to complete such tasks.

TOP: Many volunteers willingly gave of their time and talents during PCC construction.
BOTTOM: Weaving the lau to apply to the buildings.

The Vision of the Tongan Village Is Achieved

When Queen Salote learned of the Tongan Village at the PCC, she asked if a replica of her beautiful summer house might be included. This was only fitting as the Tongans are proud that their country is still a monarchy and that Tonga is the only country in Polynesia never to be colonized by a European power. Because all building funds had been allocated, the Tongan building missionaries volunteered to work on the queen's request after hours, and many Tongan residents in Lā`ie and Tongan students at the CCH supported the effort. Queen Salote aided the effort by sending two well-known tufuga to Hawai`i. Sam Langi, a child in Lā`ie at the time, said even the children would race to the Center after school to work on the queen's home.

Materials are ready to finish a Tongan hut.

Today the *Fale Fakatu`i* (Queen's House), a quarter-scale replica, stands atop a coral platform denoting the high rank of the honorary occupant. Four ironwood posts define the rectangular contours, while the ends of the fale are rounded in typical Tongan design, secured with *kafa* (sennit) lashing. It took thirty-two coconut trees to construct the decorative features on the intricate roof. The finest mats cover the floor, while the reed walls are hung with beautiful *ngatu* (tapa) portraits of Tongan royalty. The exterior is covered in reed imported from Tonga, intricately woven and tied with sennit. King Taufa`ahau Tupou IV, who visited the PCC not long after it opened, expressed his satisfaction with the Tongan Village and the replicated home of his beloved mother, Queen Salote.

Queen Salote Tupou III. She was queen from 1918 until her death in 1965.

ABOVE: *King Tupou IV and Queen Mata`aho of Tonga in 1965.*
LEFT: *Tapa interior of the queen's fale.*

Final Preparations

As the opening of the Center approached, there was some concern that the final cleanup, including window washing, would not be completed in time. The Te Arohanui Māori[4] were gathered in the CCH gymnasium for rehearsal one morning. Mike Grilikhes announced that the rehearsal that day would be postponed. Instead, said Mike, they must "do the work of the Lord in making the Center ready for the world."[5] Their instructions were to go from one end of the Center to the other, cleaning, fixing, and washing windows—doing anything else left to be done. The group accepted the responsibility that it was up to them and left immediately to walk to the Center, singing a hymn Matthew Cowley had taught them, "Be Ye Humble." They came back four or five hours later to rehearse, having finished all that needed to be done.

LANDSCAPING

Ordinarily, landscaping is done after all construction is completed. But at the PCC, the usual pattern was reversed, and trees and other plantings were done as the plants became available. Many of the coconut and breadfruit trees and numerous shrubs planted at the Center were donated by Lā`ie residents from their own yards or gardens and were replanted weekly. Other plants were propagated in a small nursery maintained by the landscaping crew.

Examples of the rare endemic flora that evolved on various Polynesian volcanic islands are found throughout the PCC, making it a botanical treasure in and of itself. These include plants the Polynesians carried with them in their voyaging canoes to use for food, clothing, and shelter in their new island homes. `Ohe (bamboo), pia (arrowroot), `awapuhi kuahiwi (wild ginger), `ulu (breadfruit tree), taro, `uala (sweet potato), and anuhe (an edible fern) thrive in the Center as do coconut and hala trees (the leaves, or lauhala, are used for weaving and plaiting).

One beloved unique tree at the Center is the niu kapakahi (crooked, or snaked coconut tree), which winds and twists across the lagoon. Mileka Apuakehau Conn donated the tree to the Center even though she could have sold it elsewhere for a lot of money. The tree grew in her Lā`ie yard where children played on it. Mileka was a labor missionary and continued working after the opening of the PCC as a quilter and a master weaver. Transplanting the large twisty tree was a challenge, but it soon became a favorite sight. In 2011 the famed niu kapakahi died and only a part of the trunk was saved, still arching over the lagoon where the original Hawaiian Village once stood.

Another useful tree found at the Center is the kukui or candlenut tree. Nuts from this tree provided light inside Hawaiian homes. The hard nuts were lightly roasted and cracked, and the oil-rich meaty kernel removed. The kernels were then threaded on the midrib of a coconut frond or on a bamboo stick and lit. Hawaiians also made lamps by shaping stones to hold the oil from the kukui nut, with a strip of tapa serving as a wick.

The `ulu, or breadfruit tree, is also found at the Center, and the fruit is another mainstay of the Polynesian diet. One mature breadfruit, which is up to ten inches in diameter and ten pounds in weight, can supply an adult with half of his or her daily nutrition, and one tree produces hundreds of fruit a year. The fruit can also be buried and fermented for long-term storage.

Central to the Hawaiian Village is the lo`i kalo, or small flooded field of taro. Taro, a tropical potato-like plant, is the Hawaiian staff of life. Cooked taro leaves taste like spinach, and the root, or corm, is pounded into poi or baked like a potato in the imu. Poi is a highly nutritious paste used as a staple food to accompany meat and fish. Still commonly eaten in Hawai`i, taro is

Transplanting the niu kapakahi, or twisted coconut tree, to the Center.

The PCC grounds have become a lush tropical garden.

*President Hugh B. Brown of the LDS First Presidency
prepares to dedicate the Polynesian Cultural Center in 1963.*

shared in the Hawaiian Village. These days taro is sometimes sliced thin and made into chips similar to potato chips.

When the labor missionaries completed their work at the Center, they had constructed the only institution of its kind then in existence—a unique showcase of some of the major island nations of the Pacific. Besides the six villages, the compound included the open-air Captain Cook Theater, the Banyan Tree Snack Bar, and a curio shop that sold native products. There were thirty-nine buildings, most of them authentic houses, council houses, and other Polynesian structures.

The labor missionaries gained a great deal personally from their service at the PCC. Besides learning English and being able to attend the Lā`ie Temple, they became proficient in their individual building trades. "They just didn't become carpenters, they became good carpenters, good builders,"[6] said Rufus Neyemihyer. Thomas Murray, who gave up a high-paying job as a policeman in New Zealand to come to Hawai`i as a labor missionary, identified another important thing the missionaries gained. "We [learned] how to tolerate the other cultures and become affiliated with them and [we learned about] their cultures. . . . [We learned from] their patience and their humility."[7]

Dedication of the Polynesian Cultural Center

On Saturday, October 12, 1963, President Hugh B. Brown, counselor to President David O. McKay in the First Presidency, presided at the dedication and grand opening of the Center. President McKay had been scheduled to come but was unable to at the last minute. About six hundred people attended the dedication, including honored guests from the state of Hawai`i and the New Zealand minister of finance. Included were representatives of all the Polynesian nations featured at the Center.

At 2 P.M., after cutting a nine-foot carnation lei and hearing a rousing rendition of the national anthem by the Royal Hawaiian Band, President Brown led the procession to the stand and the Center was officially opened. Te Arohanui Māori sang "Kia Ngawari." Speeches by visiting officials praised the great Polynesian navigators who had peopled the Pacific and said they saw in the Center a dedication to the spirit of these early explorers. Island representatives each offered responses. Noted LDS Hawaiian language and history expert, Mary Kawena Pukui, gave the final response in both Hawaiian and English.

President Brown then spoke eloquently of the brotherhood of man and the importance of education. In his dedicatory prayer he requested that "all who come here see in this Center . . . [a] better exemplification of true brotherhood."[8] This was exactly the sentiment David O. McKay felt when he witnessed the flag-raising ceremony forty-two years earlier.

Following the ceremony, dignitaries were escorted on a tour of the villages. A *Honolulu Star-Bulletin* reporter, Mary Adamski, was impressed that the labor missionaries had constructed a facility valued at $1,750,000 for a financial outlay by the Church of only $500,000.[9]

Strong words of support were written a week later by editor William H. Ewing in the same newspaper. "The Polynesian Cultural Center at Lā`ie is a project so good that adjectives fail to describe it adequately," he said. "This is a literally fantastic thing as planned and carried out by the Mormon Church. The authentic villages, the villagers at their old-time tasks, the beautiful entertainment in a wondrous setting, the education this will finance for South Pacific students at the Church College of Hawai`i—for all of this the Mormon Church deserves the highest commendation."[10]

Chiefly Titles

The PCC was uniquely honored in 1993 when Tongan King Taufa`ahau Tupou IV came to Lā`ie to bestow a chiefly title, *Mafi Fakapotu*, on then-president and CEO, Lester Moore, in an elaborate cultural ceremony. The title suggests "powerful one in the distant place," or one who is entrusted to maintain the integrity of the Tongan culture from a distance. The importance of this title is visually demonstrated in the *lakalaka*, a communal dance that represents Tongan society as a whole. At the center of the first row of dancers, the highest-ranking person in the group performs, representing the hierarchy of the Tongan kingdom. At the distant end of the long first row of dancers is the *fakapotu*, the chiefly performer who helps maintain the integrity of the front line.

Although originally bestowed on Lester Moore because he was the current president and CEO, this title stays at the Center with whoever is appointed to that office. The original authentic investiture confirms that the president and the Center are official, titled representatives of Tonga, endorsed by the king himself to portray Tongan culture.

On May 10, 1997, another chiefly title, *Galumalemana*, meaning "a powerful wave," was given to PCC president Lester Moore by His Highness Malietoa Tanumafili II, head of state of Western Sāmoa (now Sāmoa), with great ceremony.

At no other time in the history of either Sāmoa or Tonga have two heads of state travelled abroad and formally bestowed prestigious chiefly titles on a foreign person or institution. These two unprecedented honors are a strong endorsement of what the Polynesian Cultural Center is doing to preserve and display Polynesian culture. 🌿

PCC president Lester Moore receives a chiefly title from the Samoan head of state, Malietoa Tanumafili II, in 1997.

Chapter Five

Polynesia in One Place

Representatives from each village welcome guests to the PCC.

The Center presents six Polynesian villages and two displays that were added later. The villages are really small clusters of typical Polynesian houses, shelters, and buildings in a one-of-a-kind setting, where millions of visitors have learned about the history and cultures of Polynesia, all in one place. As guests stroll through the villages, they encounter smiling Polynesian students who teach them to say hello in different Polynesian languages and introduce them to the history, arts, crafts, games, and activities of the various island cultures.

Though no one actually lives in the villages, they are staffed during the day with full-time cultural specialists from each island, student demonstrators, and other part-time employees from Lā`ie and nearby Hau`ula and Kahuku, who provide specialized skills and knowledge. Everyone is there to make a visitor's day at the PCC unforgettable and as authentic as possible.

LEFT: *Harvesting coconuts.*
RIGHT: *Carved wooden tiki figure.*

The Village of Hawai'i

That the Hawaiians drew sustenance from both sea and land is illustrated in the Hawaiian Village by fishnets hanging in the sun beside the lagoon to dry and a carefully cultivated taro lo'i. Students love to explain little-known aspects of Hawaiian history from early settlement through the monarchy era as their guests enjoy the pleasant climate and gorgeous environment of Hawai'i. Greetings of aloha ring in the air.

Visitors may sample poi in the village and learn how it is made by taking their turn at pounding the root of the taro plant. They can also learn to do the hula, a dance known throughout the world for its graceful movements, and perhaps the most famous aspect of Hawaiian culture.

The hula was and is sacred to the Hawaiians as a means of preserving and passing on their history and culture. The hula was originally performed to chants and percussion instruments and later to stringed instruments and music. At one point in its history, following the entry of Western missionaries to the islands, there was a ban on all hula. The ban was lifted in 1874 by King Kalakaua who said that hula was the language of the heart, and he encouraged all his people to learn the art and teach others. Church members in Lā'ie have greatly helped to preserve and promote Hawaiian culture and traditions. Currently there is a very strong renaissance of Hawaiian culture throughout the islands.

Other Hawaiian arts on display include magnificent featherwork in the form of cloaks, aprons, helmets, lei, and *kahili,* the feather standards of royalty. The feathers were painstakingly collected by men who spent much of their time catching the preferred upland forest birds, which were virtually exterminated to meet the demand. The feathers were then tied on a network foundation, producing a texture comparable to the richest velvet. Red and yellow feathers were always preferable. One historic cape contained the feathers of about eighty thousand birds.[1]

LEFT TO RIGHT: *Kin Lo, Stan Natividad, Jimmy Bassett, Tommy Kanahele.*

Fine Hawaiian cape made from feathers.

TOP: *Wilson Ho and Vida Aiona.*
BOTTOM: *Elsie Kala* (center) *and Marilyn Aniu* (right).

James Kimo.

Bill Sproat.

Emily Kaopua.

Bill Kama on left.

Hawaiian villagers welcome guests to the Center.

Peaches Kewalo and Linda Taniguchi.

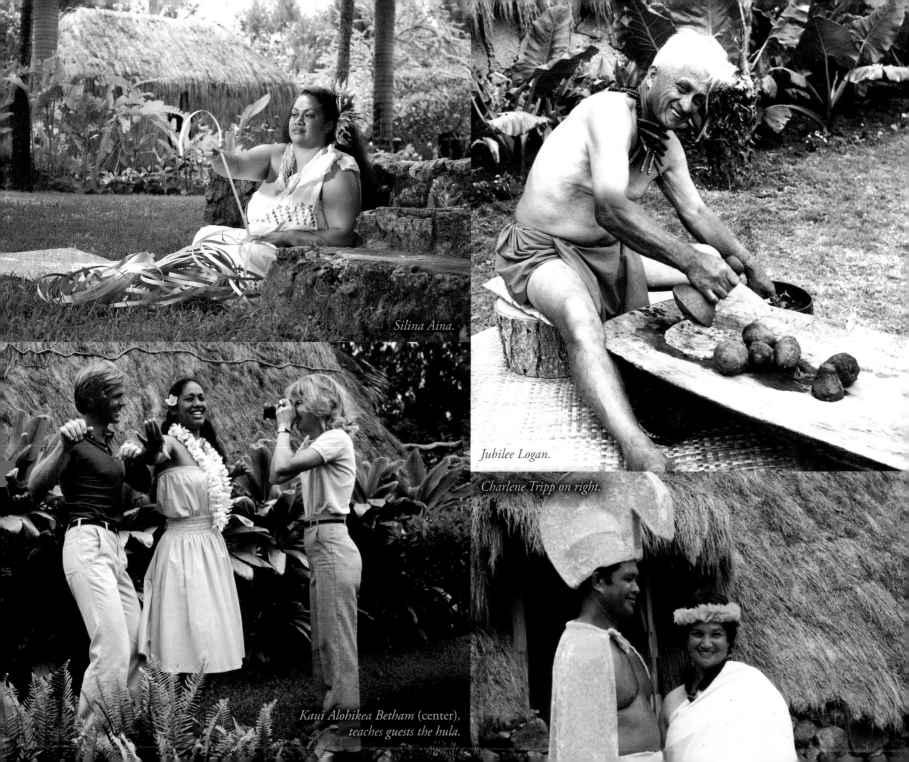

Silina Aina.

Jubilee Logan.

Charlene Tripp on right.

Kaui Alohikea Betham (center),
teaches guests the hula.

Eugenia Logan.

Tina Pasqual.

Margo Lua.

Keawe and Millie Enos.

LEFT TO RIGHT: *Alana Singh, Crystal Nagy Hafoka, Sina Nauahi Fiso.*

Keoni Ah Quin.

Demonstrating hula in the Hawaiian Village.

Terry Lei Napeahi.

Terry Panee.

Keith Awai.

Aotearoa

When PCC visitors approach the magnificently carved entrance to the village of Aotearoa, which is a Māori *pa* (a village with a stockade), they are first greeted with a *karanga* (call of recognition) by the women in the pa, whose voices are always heard first. Then a watchman wielding a *taiaha* (carved lance) appears. Posturing and grimacing menacingly, his tongue darting in and out of his tattooed face, he challenges the strangers in a formal ceremony. To discover the visitors' intent, the watchman places a *taki* (a token, usually a small carving or sprig of greenery) on the ground.

If the visitors leave the token there, they accept his challenge for battle. If they pick it up, however, they signal their peaceful intentions and are taught the traditional greeting, *kia ora*, and are welcomed with a *hongi*, the Māori greeting of pressing noses and lightly touching foreheads to exchange breath, or *hā*. This welcome ceremony, or *pōwhiri*, is reenacted many times a day at the pa.

In one corner of the village, guests join in stick games requiring concentration, coordination, and a sense of humor. Across the way, another demonstration teaches *poi*, or ball twirling, the unique skill that accompanies many Māori dances. Outside the *whare puni*, or family dwelling, women weave as they explain the distinctive red, white, and black Māori patterns worn by both men and women.

There are also explanations of the Māori art of tattooing, which is considered highly sacred and is uniquely applied by cutting grooves into the skin with fine chisels. The villagers share their knowledge of weaponry, and in the carvers' workshop, artisans sculpt and shape wood in the manner of their ancestors.

LEFT: *Guests watch demonstrations in Aotearoa.*
ABOVE: *The haka is performed on the village marae.*

Te Arohanui Maori group from New Zealand performs at the opening of the PCC in 1963.

Tommy Taurima.

Marcia Mo'o.

Angus Christy.

Shannon Niania Galea'i.

William Mahoni.

Millie Tengaio welcomes a VIP.

Varen Berryman.

Albert Whaanga.

Doe Horomona.

Nikki Wallace.

Thomas Burke.

Young warrior.   Master carver Barney Christy.

Jason Smith tattoos a young guest.

A guest practices twirling the poi balls.

Lee Gray.

George Kaka and Collin Shelford share a hongi.

The Tongan Village

In the Tongan Village guests are taught the Tongan greeting *malo e lelei* and learn more about its royal family, now headed by King Tupou VI, who suceeded to the throne in 2012 and who comes from a paramount chiefly line extending back for centuries.

The thatched buildings of the Tongan Village are distinguished by their magnificent *ngatu* (tapa). These huge sheets of layered cloth, made from the inner bark of the paper mulberry tree, are among the finest examples of this typical Polynesian art, and the process of making tapa is demonstrated in the village.

Tapa has largely been replaced by other fabric today, but it remains symbolically important in Tonga and is given at weddings, funerals, and on other ceremonial occasions.

The making of tapa is a time-consuming process. First, the bark is slit and pulled from the paper mulberry tree, yielding strips about two inches wide. These are soaked to soften the inner layer, which is separated and pounded into thin weblike membranes about a foot wide, a step that takes about forty-five minutes of continuous pounding. The strips are laid crisscross over one another and pounded together. Glue made from boiled tapioca is used to make the layers adhere to each other. This process is continued until the new tapa is the desired thickness and size. After the tapa is dried, stenciled designs using all natural black and brown dyes are applied in wonderfully varied designs.

In the village, for ceremonial everyday clothing, men and women in Tonga still wear the *ta`ovala*, a mat made of finely woven pandanus leaves tied about the waist with sennit (kafa) over other clothing. Some mats are passed down through generations as prized heirlooms.

One of the main reasons visitors find the Tongan Village memorable is the call of the Tongan drums. It has been said that when a Tongan man pounds his drum, it makes fish and birds tremble. The *tā nafa* is an exuberant drum program performed in the village and involves very large drums, large drummers, and enthusiastic visitor participation.

All village coordinators at the Center are natives from that particular country. In the early days of the PCC they were all actual male chiefs. The first exception was Tongan `Emeline `Unga, who enrolled as a student at the CCH in 1959 and became the first female village coordinator. `Emeline met her husband there and gave birth to the first Polynesian Cultural Center baby in 1963, just three months after the Center opened.

Tongan dancers welcome guests.

Una Kioa and Meliame Huakau.

Tali Taumoepeau.

Eseta Toelupe.

Two of the original tour guides at the PCC.

Dancers show their enthusiasm in Tonga.

Tevita Taumoepeau and Sione Mapa.

Tongan village hut.

Finau Lauaki Taufa helps young guest weave a fish.

Beating the drums.

Moana Fatani.

Fasi Tovo.

Solomona Toki and Soana Ngatuvai.

Drumming welcomes visitors.

John Milford on right.

The Samoan Village

The Samoan Village represents the Samoan archipelago, which lies approximately halfway between Hawai`i and New Zealand. There are actually two Sāmoas; by treaty with the high chiefs in 1900, the Stars and Stripes were raised over Tutuila and Manu`a Islands, now known as American Sāmoa. Neighboring Sāmoa (formerly known as Western Sāmoa) is an independent nation, although the two are intimately linked.

In both Sāmoas, the *matai*, or chief system, is the working social order. It is a system of behavior that has functioned well for over a thousand years. Many Samoans still live on their verdant volcanic islands much as they have for centuries, in open-sided, thatch-roofed *fale*, or oval homes, surrounding an immaculately kept *marae*, or village green. They have an instinctive joy in life that they share with friends and visitors alike. These aspects of Samoan life are evident at the PCC.

Upon entering the village, guests first learn the traditional Samoan greeting of *talofa*. Visitors are then treated to demonstrations and presentations about the coconut tree, which has always had great significance in Samoan culture.

Samoans teach visitors how coconut husking is done. First, a young Samoan dressed in a *lavalava* scampers up a forty-foot coconut tree like it is child's play. The demonstrator then illustrates the intricate art of opening a coconut to reveal the meat and milk inside.

Coconut husking is part of a Samoan's daily life, and the milk of the coconut is used to flavor most Samoan food. To open a coconut, one needs a *mele`i* (sharp stick). The first step is to thrust the soft side of the coconut onto the mele`i, and then push it downward to pop off pieces of the coconut husk. The naked coconut is held tightly in one hand and, with a hard object such as a stone, the coconut is struck across the line running between the "eyes," the shell's weakest point. If done properly, the coconut will break exactly in half, and the halves can be separated with a quick twist of the wrist, revealing the juice and coconut meat inside. Coconut milk is different from coconut juice and is rendered from shredded coconut meat. The fibers of the husk are wrapped around the shredded coconut, wringing it tightly to squeeze out the milk. This rich milk is used to flavor or marinate many of the foods of Sāmoa.

Another artful presentation that draws and holds the crowds is when the demonstrator starts a fire by rubbing two hibiscus sticks rapidly together and uses a coconut husk as tinder. Recently, a popular new attraction was added to the Samoan Village where guests, safely strapped in rock-climbing harnesses, can try coconut-tree climbing for themselves. They may also learn to weave a coconut frond sun visor.

LEFT TO RIGHT:
Tauamo Malufau, Amani Magalei, Taimi Fonoimoana, Malia Leiàtaua, Mauga Tapusoa, Faanee Tapusoa, T. David Hannemann, Muli Aumua, Pauaea Aumua.

Feagaimalir Galea`i.

Dancers perform on the village green.

Guests watch the dancing in the Samoan Village.

Falagi Soliai strips ti leaves to make leg bands.

Samoan chief's council.

Esther Dela Rosa and Uipa and Loimata Tauiliili.

Tafiti Kapeneta

Welcome to Sāmoa.

Aliese Siteine.

LEFT TO RIGHT: *Vaimalu Toilolo,
master carver Tumu Purcell, and Lagalaga Alo.*

The Fijian Village

The Fijian Village represents a nation of 322 islands spread like a horseshoe embracing the Koro Sea in the blue Pacific. The early Fijians were pottery makers as well as skilled seafarers and builders. To stabilize Fiji in 1874, the Fijians voluntarily ceded their islands to Queen Victoria of Great Britain. England ruled until Fiji's independence in 1970, although Fiji is still part of the British Commonwealth. During British rule, cotton and sugar plantations were established, and laborers from India were imported to work them. Today in Fiji, people of native descent outnumber Indians by 30 percent.

At the Center, visitors are drawn to the tall *bure kalou* (god house or spirit house), which stands dramatically against the skyline, one of the most distinctive and easy-to-spot buildings at the PCC. Inside the bure kalou, a long *masi* (tapa) banner hangs from the ridgepole and sacred spears and clubs decorate the walls. The bure kalou is one of only three of these beautiful structures in the world today.

At the entrance to the village, a fierce-looking but friendly Fijian warrior greets guests with *bula vinaka,* which means more than hello. It also conveys "good health be with you always." Visitors are invited into the Fijian dwellings, their meetinghouse, their place of work, and even their unique *vale ni qase,* or home for older people, where children are left during the day to learn Fijian legends, history, customs, and culture. The house of the chief is distinguished by the cowrie shells decorating the doorframes and the inside beams.

Demonstrations include how to make Fijian *salusalu* (lei), using dried materials tinted with natural and modern dyes. Every afternoon the student workers model the fascinating traditional Fijian dress of the nobility, the warrior class, and the common people.

Visitors are invited to participate in playing and singing Fijian style, using *derua* (bamboo instruments). The derua is held in the hand with the closed end down and struck on the ground. The tone changes with the length of the bamboo; the shorter the derua, the higher the sound, and vice versa. Another presentation is of the Fijian nose flute, which was used primarily for romance and as a means of waking the rulers of the land in the morning.

Fijian Village as seen from across the lagoon.

LEFT TO RIGHT: *Sivan Mudaliar, Emosi Damuni, and Noa Tora.*

Timoci and Velulu Sigavata.   *Naibuka Tawareguci and Toa Leiataua.*

Isireli Racule.   Nunia Sokia.

Villagers play the derua.   Bale and Tewake.

Inoke Suguturaga.

Antonio Petero.

Fijian canoe in the pageant.

Fokimoana Petero.

Meleki Turaga.

Neori Raculi.

Pierre Kimitete and young guest.

Tehina and Mahana Mōʻo.

The Tahitian Village

The Tahitian Village represents just one island in the Society Islands, a group that is part of the vast nation of French Polynesia. Today Pape`ete serves as the capital of Tahiti, and the Polynesians there speak both French as a national language and Tahitian as a national native language. With the growth of tourism, many also speak English.

In Tahiti, women still wear bright *pareau* (a wraparound dress) with fragrant flowers behind their ears, and men still fish on the reef at night and play their guitars and wooden drums. However, very few live in traditional Tahitian villages. Even on the remote islands and atolls of French Polynesia, concrete block houses have replaced thatched dwellings. Because of these changes, the Tahitian Village of the PCC is a true cultural treasure since it displays the older, authentic structures.

But the arts and crafts have not changed. One of the main presenters, Mahana Mo`o Pulotu, explains that they do almost everything in the village as it is done at home in Tahiti. She tells how the Tahitians farm fish in ingenious, highly decorated bamboo cages in the lagoon, and recounts the history of her people.

Welcomed to the village with the traditional greeting of *ia ora na*, guests are introduced to traditional Tahitian dance, a very popular attraction in the village, and one of the most dramatic in Polynesia. Years of practice are required to achieve the smooth, vibrant movement of the hips to the complex rhythm of the drums for the *tamure*, the fiery, intimate solo performance, and the *ote`a*, the dazzling line-up of dancers in tall, intricately made headdresses and grass skirts. Dancers like the weight of the skirt carried on their hips to emphasize movement. The adept drummers send distinct messages to the dancers telling them to begin specific actions, much like the caller on a square dance floor. Both men and women take part in the tamure, and visitors love to try it for themselves, even though it is very difficult.

The ankle-length skirts of the Tahitian dancers each weigh eight or nine pounds and are actually made of *fau* (wild hibiscus). The labor-intensive process of making the skirts begins with the cutting of the hibiscus. First, four- to five-foot-long branches of hibiscus are cut, and the outer bark is scraped off. The branches are tied in bundles of fifteen to twenty and immersed in the lagoon for two weeks to a month. Then the fibers are fashioned into the beautiful skirts.

Also on display is the Tahitians' own version of quilting, called *tifaifai*, which incorporates a patchwork of tiny pieces of different colored cloth into carefully arranged geometric patterns.

Tiani Mariteragi.

LEFT TO RIGHT: *Opura Mo`o,*
Tehina Mo`o, Theres Cummings.

Harry White and Aroarii Tahauri.

Tetua Tehani.

Tahitian Village performance.

Tahitian dancers in the village.

LEFT TO RIGHT: *Kameron Ho Ching, Tahitoe Carlson, Kory Pace.*

Tahitian Village on the lagoon.

Weaving baskets in the Tahitian Village.

LEFT TO RIGHT: *Jimmy Bassett,
Patoa Benioni, Vave Leauanae.*

Rene Tetuanui (left) and Sylvand Tahauri (right).

Raymond Mariteragi.

Clint Mariteragi.

The Marquesas Village

The Marquesas Village was not one of the original PCC villages but was added in 1973 as an exhibit only, because of its significance as part of the Polynesian triangle. The Marquesas are the largest island group in French Polynesia but are little known by the outside world today. Decimated by the introduction of Western diseases and weapons, the population in 1920 was only 1,200 people. By then the culture was almost completely stripped of its traditions. Slow to recover, the current population is a mere 10,000. Most Marquesans have never left their home island.

The exhibit is modeled after a chief's ceremonial compound that was on a high stone *tohua* (platform) that once existed on the island of Nuku Hiva and typifies life during the late eighteenth century. The chief's house, the *ha`e haka`i*, is at one end of the tohua. The PCC tohua is about a tenth the size of an actual tohua and is constructed of coral rather than the basalt rock the Marquesans would have used in their homeland. Though small in size, the compound is accurate in detail thanks to Dr. Yoshiko Sinoto, an anthropologist at Honolulu's Bishop Museum, who spent much time in the Marquesas uncovering major archeological excavations. Pierre Kimitete, a Marquesan who lived in Hawai`i in 1973, did much of the carving in the Marquesan compound.

In the 1980s, artist Eriki Marchand came to BYU–H from Tahiti. He had served a mission in the Marquesas and so became the Marquesas Village manager. Eriki invigorated the village by designing costumes, writing scripts, and teaching dances. For the first time Marquesas became a living village where visitors could observe the *haka puaka* (pig hunting dance) and learn fun and interesting facts about the Marquesas. After Eriki left, the Marquesas Village continued to be a living village on and off as a few more

Marquesan students found their way to Lā`ie. In 2009, because of budget constraints in a difficult economy, the village reverted back to its original exhibit-only status. In the future the tohua will be used as a special events site, but the hope is that it might eventually be restored as a fully operational cultural attraction.

Tahitoe Carlson.

Marquesan tohua at the PCC.

Peter Tovey.

Carved figures of the Marquesas.

Tom Mariteragi.

Carved moai at the PCC, showing the completed eyes.

The Rapa Nui (Easter Island) Exhibit

Rapa Nui, or Easter Island, is considered to be the loneliest outpost of Polynesia. When Captain James Cook sailed there in 1774, he saw for himself the gigantic stone *moai* (monuments), which are fifteen to thirty feet high. Some wore *pukao* (red stone hats). The moai stand on *ahu* (altar platforms) ten to twelve feet high. These massive, eerie sentinels, facing the island interior and surrounding its perimeter, are recognized across the world as icons of Polynesia.

A combination of slave raids, war, famine, and the introduction of Western diseases depopulated Rapa Nui. By 1871 there were only 111 *Rapanui* (natives) in existence. In a society based on oral tradition, the loss was catastrophic. The traditional ways of life were essentially gone.

At the PCC, Rapa Nui is represented as an exhibit built around a centerpiece of five stone moai. Sergio Rapu, Rapa Nui's first native governor, brought four Rapanui stone masons to the PCC to carve and install the display. The moai were carved from enormous blocks of concrete injected with air bubbles to replicate Rapa Nui's volcanic stone. The concrete proved to be so similar in texture, color, and durability that the carvers could scarcely tell the difference.

Using axes, chisels, power sanders, and even a traditional Easter Island *toki*, or adze, the carvers soon produced the distinctive faces of the moai. The perfect red scoria rock, or volcanic slag, was found on Moloka`i to create the pukao. Even at half the size of the originals, the completed statues each weigh two tons. After twelve years of planning and execution, five enormous moai now stand as sentinels on Coconut Island in the Center's lagoon where the exhibit was installed. Two more lie on the grass as if unfinished.

Anticipating the important eye-placing ceremony that would "make the moai come alive," the carvers dived to the ocean floor before leaving Easter Island to find the best white coral and shells for the moai eyes. At noon on February 3, 2003, according to ancient ritual, the eye-placing ceremony was enacted.

Other exhibits in the display tell about the lost Easter Island culture. Although no trees grow on the wind-blown island, archeologists now know that the island was once forested. When wood was available, houses were built of wood on stone platforms. In the PCC exhibit, the *hare vaka* (house), which represents this early phase, is purposely left open and exposed so its unique construction, which resembles an overturned canoe, can be appreciated. Scholars think this aerodynamic form was developed because of the harsh winds that constantly sweep across the island. The old dwellings were often thirty to sixty feet long, some more than three hundred feet long. After the trees were all gone, the people were forced to build their houses entirely of stone. The *hare maea* (stone house) is a fine example of this type of dwelling. Structures to protect the staple crops of banana, taro, sugarcane, and sweet potato from the wind were also built. The *mana vai* (agricultural enclosure) consists of rock walls surrounding a growing area that helps the plants gather and retain water during the dry summer months.

LEFT: *Moai lying on ground unfinished.*
TOP: *Easter Island house.*
BOTTOM: *Upright moai.*

Canoes

All Polynesian cultures had advanced watercraft in the form of single- or double-hulled outrigger canoes with triangular sails, usually woven from pandanus. Because fish were a key part of the Polynesian diet, most Polynesian families had at least one canoe. This is reflected at the Center, where villages have canoe houses to protect the canoes from sun and saltwater, and where many wonderful canoes are on display.

One special canoe is the fifty-seven-foot *waka taua*, or Māori war canoe. A war canoe was the primary symbol of tribal power in Aotearoa. When fitted with sails, these canoes could cover great distances with considerable speed. Hulls were as long as one hundred feet and could hold up to ninety-five warriors. Construction of a waka taua was begun in New Zealand for the visit of King George V of England in 1936, but the king died, and the unfinished canoe was left in the forest and used as a watering trough. Years later the canoe project was resurrected with the idea of displaying the waka taua at the Center. The unfinished canoe was shipped to Hamilton, New Zealand, where it became part of the greater carving project for the Center. Master woodcarver Bill Whautapu was found to guide them. He insisted that the canoe first be filled with water. As he carefully observed the rising water, he marked high spots inside the canoe. After it was emptied and dried, the carvers carved out the high spots, making it evenly balanced.

In 1962, the waka taua, named *Te ika roa a Maui* (Maui's long fish), was finished under the direction of *tufuga whakairo* (master carver) Piri Poutapu in time for the PCC opening in 1963. This waka taua, carved from a single *kauri* tree, is approximately sixty feet long and weighs two and a half tons.

In the 1980s, the Polynesian Institute and the PCC commissioned a large, double-hulled, ocean-voyaging *camakau* (Fijian canoe). According to Fijian protocol, the canoe had to be commissioned by Prime Minister Ratu Sir Kamisese Mara, who also formally presented the camakau to the Center upon its completion. The camakau was carved in Fiji from a single log, using only indigenous materials. It is one of the few, if not the only, remaining camakau in the world.

Another canoe displayed at the Center is a beautiful Samoan *va'aalo*, or tuna fishing canoe. Guests watched its progress as it was carved by master carver Tumu Tapusoa Purcell, who came to Lā'ie as a labor missionary. Tumu, the master carver for the Samoan Village, carved the canoe from a single koa log he found on the island of Hawai'i. When the canoe was finished in 1989,

Women doing a poi dance while standing in the waka taua.

the villagers enthusiastically hoisted it onto their shoulders and carried it to the lagoon for its inaugural voyage.

In display cases at the entrance to the Center is a wonderful collection of model Polynesian canoes crafted by master carver Tui`one Pulotu that shows the wide variations among the canoes of the various islands.

But the masterpiece of canoes at the Center is the fifty-seven-foot-long, twin-hulled Hawaiian voyaging canoe called *Iosepa.* Master carvers Tui`one Pulotu and Kawika Eskaran carved *Iosepa* in less than seven months without drawings of any kind, sometimes working around the clock. Built under the auspices of the Jonathan Napela Center for Hawaiian and Pacific Island Studies (formerly the Polynesian Institute) at BYU–H, with funding from the W. K. Kellogg Foundation, the project became a community effort, with people coming from all over Oahu and even other islands to help. Throughout the project, students were not only trained in canoe carving but in sailing techniques as well.

Iosepa was launched on Hukilau Beach on November 3, 2001, amid great tradition, ceremony, and fanfare. Dedicated by Elder M. Russell Ballard, *Iosepa* is housed in a special canoe house, the *Hale Wa`a,* in the Hawaiian Village, where guests can inspect and learn about it. It is a floating classroom for BYU–H instruction, and it sails each spring term to give students ocean experience with ancient sailing methods.

Canoes also serve a very practical role at the Center, giving groups of guests the option to ride down the lagoon and view the villages from the water. Recently, individual canoe rides have been offered to guests who may paddle themselves down the lagoon. In addition, whenever the villages at the PCC have had to be moved to different locations, the Polynesian buildings have been placed on canoes and floated down the lagoon to their new sites.

TOP: *The* Iosepa *is used as a floating classroom by BYU–Hawai`i.*
BOTTOM: *Canoe on the lagoon at the PCC.*

TOP: *Lily Kama* (left).
BOTTOM: *Lily Kama and Lucy `Unga, master quilters.*

Mission Settlement chapel at the PCC.

Hawaiian Mission Settlement

Over the years the Center has added other attractions that enhance the cultural lectures and demonstrations in the villages and help visitors experience more of Polynesia. One such attraction is the Hawaiian Mission Settlement, which was opened in 1984 to honor and celebrate the heroic sacrifices of all the Christian missionaries that had come to the islands, be they Protestant, Catholic, or Latter-day Saint. The complex includes a stone mission home, a schoolhouse, and a nondenominational chapel, all reminiscent of the buildings built by the missionaries. A bell from the historic LDS Pulehu chapel on Maui is in the chapel belfry. The settlement is a quiet oasis where visitors can rest or study displays documenting the great efforts of the early Christian missionaries.

Hawaiian quilts are prominently displayed in the mission home. Taught to quilt by the female missionaries, the Hawaiians received their inspiration from shapes found in nature and stitched them in the undulating pattern of ocean waves. The early quilts were bold adaptations using an appliqué rather than a pieced technique and are considered heirlooms and treasures today. Kits to try Hawaiian quilting may be purchased in the mission home.

Hukilau Theater

Another addition to the Center is the large-format Hukilau Theater (originally the IMAX Theater), which opened in 1991 after a dedication service by President Thomas S. Monson, then a counselor in the LDS First Presidency. It was the first large-format theater in Hawai`i. With a screen sixty-five feet high and

Mission Settlement across the lagoon.

ninety-six feet wide, viewers sit in steeply tiered rows, which bring the screen closer to the audience and enhance the perception of being in the picture.

Academy award-winning filmmaker, Kieth Merrill, was commissioned by the PCC to produce and direct *Polynesian Odyssey* for the new theater, which aired regularly, along with other films, for the first twenty years. Shot on location all over Polynesia, *Polynesian Odyssey* transports viewers across the Pacific and dramatizes the exploration and population of the islands.

The Hukilau Theater is being renovated to look as if an ancient volcano engulfed it, making it even more dramatic and enjoyable. When renovations are complete, guests will feel as if they are walking through a lava tube to enter the theater. The exterior will be turned into the mountainous slopes of the volcano, with rock walls and two waterfalls. A new film is being produced that will tell the story of little-known aspects of Hawai`i. The renovated theater and new movie will feature an HD system with 4,096-line resolution and a robust new sound system to complement the imagery, and will debut late in 2012.

Tour of Lā`ie

Another popular activity guests can enjoy is the tour of Lā`ie. There is no proselytizing by The Church of Jesus Christ of Latter-day Saints at the Center, despite the fact that the Church sends missionaries all over the world. In fact, many visitors learn of the Church association only in casual conversation, and many never learn of it at all. However, for those curious about the history of the community and its association with the Church, there is a free thirty-five-minute tram tour through Lā`ie. The tour passes the

Trolley taking guests on a tour of Lā`ie.

campus of BYU–Hawai`i and proceeds to the temple visitors' center. Although only LDS members in good standing are permitted to enter the temple itself, displays, videos, and films at the adjacent visitors' center welcome guests and introduce them to the basic principles of the Church, which include a strong emphasis on the importance of the family and living a moral and upright life. Inside the visitors' center, a sixteen-foot-high statue of the resurrected Jesus Christ invites quiet contemplation. Inspirational recordings can be heard in twenty-eight languages.

In 1958, when David O. McKay said that tens of millions of people would come to Lā`ie to discover its significance, many wondered how that could happen in such a small place. With the gift of hindsight, it is clear that the Polynesian Cultural Center has been the vehicle in bringing this to pass. President Gordon B. Hinckley confirmed that the only way President McKay's prophetic statement could be realized was through the Polynesian Cultural Center and the visitors it attracts. He called the Center "a most remarkable and unusual phenomenon."[2] In 2011, the total visitor count at the PCC had reached 37 million. ❧

Chapter Six

Night Show

The Captain Cook Theater on opening night 1963.

In the absence of written languages, music became the expression of the soul of Polynesia, and songs, dances, and chants have preserved the history of the people, telling of myths, migrations, gods, heroes, wars, love, and marriage. The Polynesian music explained the universe, recorded genealogies, and passed down values and morals from generation to generation. In Polynesia, the human body became an extension of the music, an instrument expressing emotion or imitating the rhythms of nature like a waving palm, the surf kissing the shore, the arc of the sun crossing the sky, or a bird in motion. In its highest form, the dance was also a type of prayer.

The implements of Polynesian music and dance are many. They include sharkskin-topped drums, gourd rattles, nose flutes, smooth stones hit together, split bamboo, bamboo tubes, hollow gourds, and rhythm sticks. The materials for these ancient implements were gathered from nature and then skillfully fashioned. After Western contact, stringed instruments such as guitars were introduced and adapted. The small Portuguese mandolin called the *braguinha* became the world-famous `ukulele, literally a "jumping flea," in Hawaiian hands. Cracker tins and gasoline barrels in Tonga morphed into metal drums.

The night show at the PCC has always aimed to present the best of Polynesian music and dance as authentically as possible. In its first forty years of operation, the Center staged almost twenty different productions. One early program featured an incredible fifty-eight numbers, almost more than the audience could digest. A later version, *Horizons! Where the Sea Meets the Sky,* presented forty numbers, each portraying a different culture, style, or message. In the beginning, the night show program changed often because publicists always wanted something new to advertise. Eventually producers realized that the transient nature of tourism meant that the audience pool changed so rapidly new scripts weren't necessary. With time, though, this supposition changed again as more and more repeat visitors came to Hawai`i and wanted to see different things.

Captain Cook Theater

A theater was an integral part of plans for the PCC right from the initial concept, and the Captain Cook Theater was built by the labor missionaries. Originally seating 600 people, it was expanded a few years later to 750, and finally to about 1,300 by adding bleachers on the side. The concept was imaginative and romantic, befitting the allure of Polynesia. The semicircular stage resembled an island with a three-foot-deep lagoon or moat around

Hawaiian dancers perform in the opening show.

the outside of the apron. Instead of a traditional velvet curtain, water jets around the lagoon, illuminated by colored footlights, shot twenty feet into the air from the lip of the stage on cue, masking transitions as surely as a curtain.

Behind the grass-covered performance area, a gas-operated thirty-eight-foot-high, simulated volcano roared with flames and smoke on command, while four electric pump-driven waterfalls splashed down the rocks. *Tiki* (an image or statue) and verdant tropical plantings provided a rich ambiance of island splendor. It was the most beautiful and elaborate stage setting for music and dance in Hawai`i.

Originally the sound system consisted of a sealed sound booth and microphones suspended from a single cable running the length of the stage. And the lighting system was one light switch—on or off. As this soon proved to be inadequate, Michele (Mike) Grilikhes brought in a team of Hollywood specialists to upgrade the sound and lighting systems to professional standards.

Grilikhes had been a consultant to the Center before it opened and essentially directed the first night show. Later he managed the Center for several months. He was a relatively new member of the Church, married to film star Laraine Day (who was also a member

Mike Grilikhes and his wife, Laraine Day, with President Hugh B. Brown at the dedication of the Center in 1963.

of the Church). Although he knew almost nothing about Polynesia, his nine years at CBS television as a producer and director gave him a good idea of what it would take to create a professional show.

Grilikhes's team included Joseph Southworth, a sound coordinator, and lighting expert Lard Davis. Irving Sudrow was hired to train the stage managers. Jack Regas, a professional choreographer with Hollywood experience, was employed to perfect staging and help the performers become more precise and professional in their transitions. Every effort was made to be truly authentic in the songs, dance steps, and costume elements, but professional attention was given to the presentation and staging to make it more pleasing for the audience. Grilikhes repeatedly assured the dancers he would never change any of their dance steps—just the staging.[1] Some critics thought it was too "show biz," but the hope was that the compromise always erred on the side of authenticity.

The First Night Show

A Night through Polynesia, the first PCC night show, was inspired by Wylie Swapp's *Polynesian Panorama,* which had been so successful in Waikiki. Besides the students from the CCH, other performers were enlisted to enhance the first night show. Grilikhes went to New Zealand to evaluate the Te Arohanui Māori entertainers. Mike and Laraine Grilikhes were deeply moved by what they saw in New Zealand. He reported that the performers were people right out of the villages—old, young, and middle-aged. Mike said, "It was beautiful. The voices were magnificent,"[2] and that there was no cultural performing group any place in the world that could compare to them in the beauty and skill of performance. Te Arohanui Māori proceeded with plans to come to Hawai`i.

Editor's Note: The Polynesian Cultural Center is presenting "A Night Through Polynesia" every evening at 8 except Sundays through the summer months. Bob Paulos, publisher of the Hawaii PRESS Newspapers, wrote the following in his "Bobbin' Around With Bob Paulos" column, which appears regularly in the PRESS community papers.

From the first appearance of the fountain "curtain" and the gorgeous lighting of the first segment I was completely captivated by "A Night Through Polynesia," the summer festival presentation at the Polynesian Cultural Center at Laie.

This is one of the most entertaining and educational shows I've ever had the pleasure of seeing and as they say in the trade I'm a "tough audience." I'm not the best tourist in the world. I don't enjoy the browsing and touring and sightseeing that makes a good visitor or vacationer...that is, I didn't until I came to Hawaii.

Maybe I'm getting older or my tastes are changing, but I don't believe so. I believe that Hawaii just has so much more to offer than anyplace else that a person can't help himself.

And one of the greatest attractions I've found to date is the show at the PCC. The six segments—each about 20 minutes long— take the spectator to the Hawaii of old, to Tonga, Tahiti, Fiji, Samoa and Maori. The history and culture of these islands is revealed in songs and dances by extremely talented performers.

Making Spoons for Polynesian Pupu

But the overall professional quality of the presentation and lighting adds a quality to the show for which I was totally unprepared. I saw the premiere performance of the new summer show as an invited guest and went politely to my seat. I was happy to notice that there would be an intermission halfway through and plotted an inconspicuous escape after the first half of the revue. But it would have taken wild horses, as the saying goes, to drag me out of there before the performance ended.

After driving home I was up till after 1 a.m. reading volumes of the encyclopedia for additional information on these islands. For the night at least I became some kind of a nut on Polynesian culture...and I have the feeling that this show is so extraordinarily good that it will have the same effect on everyone who sees it.

Not the least of the qualities of the presentation are the excellent acoustics of the amphitheatre...

thrilling voices of the male chorus of Fiji Islanders and the showmanship of their leader—the beautiful headdresses

Young Dancers at the Center

of the Samoan dancers, and the lovely Maori music—I would find it impossible to describe the beauty of the show.

Michel M. (Mike) Grilikhes has taken over direction of the center and lighting and direction of the show is by Jack Regas. Years of experience for both men in movie and television production is evident in their first production. It's a must for everyone in Hawaii...as well as all of our visitors.

Aside from the show itself the visitor to the PCC is in for a treat at the "Polynesian Pupu," a sort of South Pacific smorgasbord which is served each evening at the center. If anyone had told this flat-land midwesterner a few years back that he'd be sitting on the floor eating "mao fafa" or "paraowa rewena" you can bet your life he wouldn't have believed it, but that was part of the menu.

The pupu is made up of foods native to each of the six cultures represented in the villages at the center. As the visitor tours each of the villages before the pupu he can watch the food being prepared exactly as it would be on that island.

Here is the menu from each village:

Hawaiian—Kalua pua'a (roast pork), kamano lomi-lomi (pickled salmon), haupia (coconut dessert).

Tahitian—Poe iita (papaya pudding), moa fafa (chicken with taro leaves and coconut milk), eia ota (raw fish).

Tongan—Kumala (sweet potato), faikakai (taro pudding), otai (fruit cocktail).

Samoan—Talo tao (baked taro with coconut milk) palusami (baked taro leaves), niu (coconut juice.).

Maori—(New Zealand)—Paraowa rewena (leavened bread), purini (fruit pudding), kaimoana (sea food salad.).

Fijian—Bulu makau rourou (corned beef with taro leaves and coconut milk), ura vakalolo (shrimps with taro leaves and coconut leaves), sivaro maca (taro in grated coconut sauce).

The menu was not only interesting, but quite enjoyable.

I'm no drama critic or reviewer of plays nor am I gourmet—but I know when I thoroughly enjoy myself and I surely did at the PCC. I think you will, too. Try it.

The Center received good publicity when it opened in 1963.

Then Fijian Isireli Racule volunteered to bring his Fijian dance company to the opening celebration. The night show was shaping up to exceed all expectations.

Preparations for opening night were intense until the last minute. The control panel that operated the new sound and light systems didn't arrive until the afternoon of opening day. They learned that it was sitting on a ship in Honolulu harbor. Electricians were actually connecting wires minutes before the show began. Stage manager Larry Nielson remembered that the water curtain was running all right, but the waterfall wasn't working. "We did a lot of praying,"[3] said Grilikhes. That it all came together as the show opened was, in his mind, a miraculous thing.

Opening night was October 12, 1963. The crowd overflowed the Captain Cook Theater and several hundred had to sit on folding chairs hastily set up on the stage apron beneath a misty spray from the water curtain and within swishing distance of the Tahitian skirts. There were seven hundred performers in the show that night, about the same number as in the audience.[4] When the show erupted in all its color, energy, and pageantry, the effect was electric and the audience applauded wildly. Two hours later everyone, performers and guests, was elated and spiritually moved. Nielson said, "To see a dream come true before my eyes was something I'll never forget."[5]

When the show began, the curtain did not rise to a chorus of trumpets and the ruffle of drums. Fittingly, it began with the mellow notes of conch shells calling all to gather as the stars blazed low over Lā`ie and the trade winds blew gently off the sea. Each part of the show provided an introduction to the distinctive music and dance of the various Polynesian cultures. Every minute was full of interest and excitement. Even after two hours of performance, including a fireknife dance by Tafili Galea`i, it all seemed to end

Samoan dancers perform in the opening show.

Finale of Horizons! showing the water curtain around the stage in the Pacific Theater.

too soon. When it was over the audience went wild, spontaneously leaping to their feet with cheers and a long ovation. At the end of the applause, the Fijian dancers all jumped into the lagoon, eliciting more rounds of applause.

There have been many versions of the night show since then, including *Invitation to Paradise*, *This Is Polynesia*, and *Mana, The Spirit of Our People*. The night show became the premier Polynesian entertainment not only in Hawai`i, but in the whole Pacific. By the 1970s, tickets were at such a premium that tour agents made reservations months in advance. To accommodate growing crowds, double shows were scheduled on many evenings.

Pacific Theater

Over the years refinements were made to the Captain Cook Theater to accommodate growing demand, but eventually the theater had to be replaced altogether. In February 1976, the new Pacific Theater debuted, with seating for 2,500 guests. Three years later it was expanded to seat 2,775. The Pacific Theater, which still serves the PCC, is a larger version of the Captain Cook Theater, which was so successful. An eighty-foot cantilevered roof rises above the performance area to keep the audience and dancers dry in case of rain.

The theater has undergone other changes and upgrades over the years. When the show *Horizons!* was created in 1995, the vibrant production necessitated changes to the stage itself. The floor surface was layered with foam, plywood, and carpet over the cement slab, the latest in performance technology, to minimize shin splints and body stress for the dancers.

Backstage Efforts

One of the reasons the night show has been such a grand spectacular over the years is the beautiful costuming. New costumes are constructed by a small but highly dedicated and trained wardrobe staff for every version of the night show. The costume people are divided into two divisions, the regular tailors and seamstresses, and those who specialize in the construction of the traditional parts of the wardrobe—the feathers, shells, bone, and natural fibers. Native costumes are thoroughly researched for authenticity in their home islands, in the Pacific Collection at BYU–Hawai`i Library, and at

TOP: *Costumes are kept clean and ready for the performers.* LEFT: *One of many seamstresses who have created hundreds of costumes over the years, Faatu Talataina works diligently.*

Dizzying scenes from the early night shows, Invitation to Paradise, *and* This Is Polynesia.

Scenes from Horizons! Where the Sea Meets the Sky.

A light and sound technician works behind the scenes.

Honolulu's Bishop Museum. Seamstresses are constantly sewing, repairing, replacing, and creating new costumes, and outfitting new performers. When *Horizons!* debuted, more than 400 new costumes were created for 120 cast members.

Keeping the costumes clean and fresh is another huge daily effort. A complete laundry facility delivers fresh, clean costumes every night on a large conveyor belt. Each performer has a spot marked on the belt and gathers his or her costumes for the evening performance. The props, implements, and instruments also require special care. The big drums, for example, are stored in a special room with hot lights to keep the skins dry and taut.

A look backstage at the night show reveals the complexity of nightly preparations and the number of unsung heroes who labor behind the scenes. There are carpenters, stage crews, prompters, technicians, sound and light crews, electricians, and prop people. They are the ones who light the torches, handle the fireknives, get the volcano erupting, and push the huge drums on stage. They're all part of the technical services department numbering approximately forty workers, 70 percent of whom are students. Technical services is also responsible for the sound for the canoe pageant in the afternoon, and sound and lighting for the Ali`i Luau before the night show.

The Performers

The performers and technical specialists are primarily students carrying a full academic load at BYU–H. While Polynesian students perform on stage, backstage responsibilities are often handled by non-Polynesian students. Many of them also have responsibilities in the Church, which has no paid ministry and relies on its members to fill roles as teachers and administrators. Their jobs at the Center enable them to pay tuition and support themselves while they gain an education.

About 2,500 students, representing more than seventy countries, attend BYU–H each year, and a large percentage of them are enrolled in the IWork scholarship program, available to all international students.[6] A scholarship provides 50 percent grant and 50 percent forgivable loan, if, after graduation, the recipient returns to their geographical area to live, work, and contribute there. Scholarship recipients are required to work. At the PCC, they can perform in the night show, be tour guides or demonstrators in the villages, or do other work for nineteen hours each week. Paid an hourly wage, they receive 40 percent of their earnings in a regular paycheck. The other 60 percent is deducted from their paychecks and goes to BYU–H to help cover tuition.

Another mission of the Center is to plant Polynesian culture in the hearts, minds, and souls of the Polynesian students. They learn their own music, dance, and culture at the Center. In addition, many learn the music and dance of cultures other than their own. There, perhaps for the first time, they meet and interact with other Polynesians and learn of their greater collective heritage. This knowledge gives the students great strength and courage. Debbie Hippolite Wright, who went on from student performer to become a BYU–H professor and is now a vice president at BYU–H,

PCC employees hard at work in the Center.

explained it this way: "Māoris have a term called *turangawaewae,* a place of standing. You have to know where you stand, where you come from, in order to stand strong. . . . If I know . . . my place of standing in the gospel, in my family, in my tribe, in my community, in my professional world, then I'm going to . . . make a contribution."[7]

The show demands great physical conditioning and stamina. Dancers, like athletes before a game, warm up and stretch out before each show. They go through weeks of training and rehearsal before they face an audience, and they are worked into the show gradually as they perfect each dance.

They also prepare themselves mentally before each show when the entire cast, including all of the support people, gathers for a short meeting. A student shares information about his or her home island, a spiritual thought on a gospel subject, or an idea for self-improvement. A cast member offers a prayer that may include a plea for safety and a hope that the performers will do their best to share truth and beauty with all who have come. Then it's curtain time.

The Fireknife Dance

The showstopper of the evening show is often the fireknife dance. The *siva naifi afi,* or the `*ailao afi* (the twirling of fire), is the most dramatic dance in Polynesia. Although the dance, performed with a hook knife, is ancient in origin, the fire on the end of the knife is a Hollywood-style innovation. While the drums beat faster and louder, a single dancer twirls a fireknife lit at both ends. He spins circles of flames—over the head, between his legs, at arm's length, and high in the air while standing and lying on the stage. He even hurls the fireknife, spearlike, to a waiting warrior perched on the volcano. Others join the dancer until there are six of them twirling in unison.

Pulefano Galea`i learned fireknife dancing from his sister Vatau, who won a Miss Sāmoa title in Hawai`i because of her talent as a fireknife dancer. He went on to dance in the night show. Galea`i emphasized that it's not really twirling the knife that counts, but the showmanship of the performance. He taught a team of twelve boys to do the fireknife under the direction of Amani Magalei in 1967. This team, including Tiueni Purcell, Pisona Tenaga, Lisona Leiataua, and Talafua, performed to rave reviews at the Hollywood Bowl and in Salt Lake City. Visitors often ask if the flames are real or if the young men wear skintight asbestos suits. How can anyone play with fire and not be burned? they want to know.

Performers attend a brief motivational meeting before the show goes on.

Pisona Tevaga performs the first
fireknife dance at the night show.

TOP: *Group fireknife dance.*
BOTTOM: *Fire walk.* LEFT TO RIGHT: *Samiu Fineanganofo, Paina Mikaele, Boyd Lauano.*

It takes a great deal of courage to also take part in the *savali afi*, or the fire walk. Here the men do a contemporary version of the ancient practice of walking barefoot across glowing hot stones. They sit on the flames, jump up with their leaf skirts smoking, and then sit down again. Finally, they master the flames by sitting on the fire altogether, suffocating the flames completely.

HĀ—BREATH OF LIFE

By the early 2000s, the night show *Horizons! Where the Sea Meets the Sky* had been playing for over a decade. After a great deal of work, *Hā—Breath of Life* became the new night show, and *Horizons!* was retired after a successful fourteen-year run.

Production of the new show proceeded at a deliberate, measured pace. With the help of consultant David Warner, cultural committees were organized to identify core values, an enlightening and valuable process. Producer Delsa Moe said, "It was like opening up these layers [of an onion] that got down to [our] true identity that had somehow been lost."[8]

Each committee decided which core values could be portrayed on stage, and Warner suggested they develop a storyline with a central character that the audience could relate to and that would have universal appeal. The plot follows the life of a boy, Mana, from the time he is born, through his life, to the birth of his own daughter, a lifetime set within Polynesian cultures and core values. Before *Hā—Breath of Life,* this kind of Polynesian show had never been done before.

The island cultures are still represented as backdrops to Mana's life story. The Tongans welcome him as a new baby, and Hawai`i celebrates his survival with feasting and hula. The Māori help Mana develop into a man. In Sāmoa he must literally walk through fire to prove his love for the beautiful young Lani, and the

Logo Atu Vaka as the father in
Hā–Breath of Life.

*Tupi Tupou and Logo Atu Vaka welcome
a child in* Hā–Breath of Life.

Scenes from Hā–Breath of Life.

David Galea`i performing a fireknife dance.

Kalivati Volavola.

Tahitians mark their marriage ceremony with joyous celebration. In Fiji, Mana defends his home and mourns the death of his father. As the cast comes together for the finale, everyone celebrates the first breath of Hina, Mana and Lani's new daughter—the circle of life.

New techniques were introduced to help move the story forward and transition the story from section to section. One was animation. A visiting BYU–Provo film professor, Ryan Woodward, had used animation to tell the Samoan legend of the turtle and the shark. His drawings looked like Polynesian tapa cloth, art come to life. Professor Woodward and his company were subsequently recruited to prepare supporting animation for *Hā*. Two screens, shaped like Polynesian canoe sails, are mounted on either side of the stage for the animated segments. Now, regardless of what language a guest speaks, they can follow the storyline using three different cues—the narration, the animation, or the action on stage.

Animation motif for
Hā–Breath of Life.

Before the opening of *Hā,* 120 students had to be trained, and over 2,000 new costumes had to be made. Alterations were made to the Pacific Theater to accommodate the new production. In an effort to draw the audience in and make the stage look more like an island, the water curtain was eliminated and a sandy beach was built right up to the front row seats. Performers now used the whole theater as a stage, moving up and down the aisles freely. A state-of-the-art surround-sound system was installed to provide better clarity.

Sections of the new show were worked into *Horizons!,* the old night show, for audience tests, and they were received enthusiastically. Finally, *Hā–Breath of Life* was launched on August 14, 2009, and it became an immediate success. During 2010, the new show helped increase the PCC visitor count significantly. Some compared it to Disney's *The Lion King,* and others thought, with its lavish staging and costuming, it was like a Broadway production. One visitor who watched *Hā–Breath of Life* summed up his experience this way: "I have traveled the world and seen productions and performances in New York, Brazil, Paris, Rome, and Washington, DC. . . . However, none of them surpass the performance of *Hā–Breath of Life.* That show left me breathless and speechless."[9]

Night after night, *Hā–Breath of Life* performs to full houses and receives standing ovations. In 2011, market research showed that one-third of the guests coming to the PCC come primarily to see the new production.

The night show, no matter what the name, has been a continuing success for almost fifty years. One performer in the first night show could speak for the millions who have sat in the audience or performed on stage. "Man alive! The night show just pulsates through your whole system. It is one of the most dramatic experiences—tremendously moving!" ❧

Chapter Seven

Road to Success

POLYNESIAN CULTURAL CENTER
Open Daily (except Sunday)
from 10 a.m. to 5 p.m.

Adul ADMISSION
        Children under 12.. 75¢
    pecial Evening Performances
  or Information Call 299-207 or 299-2

-PROFIT ACTIVITY of the Pacific Board of Education of the Church of Jesus Christ of Latter Day

Actor Henry Fonda (top center) *participates in activities while visiting the PCC.*

Actor Kirk Douglas (left) *is greeted with a hongi.*

Jacqueline Kennedy (bottom center), *former first lady, makes a surprise visit to the PCC in 1966.*

Popular television personality
Art Linkletter (center) *is honored at the PCC.*

Rave reviews accompanied the opening of the PCC in 1963, and euphoria powered the first weeks of operation. However, the Fijiian and Māori dance troupes had to return to their homes, leaving the resident 150 PCC students to carry on, most of whom were new to the entertainment business. It was one thing to construct the Center, but another to regularly fill it with guests. Audience size at the night show, which was only presented once or twice a week, plummeted. Some nights the cast greatly outnumbered the audience. Other times shows were cancelled because of low attendance.

The student performers did everything they could to attract patrons. Cast members and Lā`ie villagers parked their cars in the Center parking lot to give the illusion of crowds. They lined up along Kamehameha Highway to attract attention, dancing, smiling and waving to passing cars and tour buses. Carloads of costumed dancers drove to Waikiki to walk the beach and spread the word. In their eagerness to have the PCC succeed, students even worked for free and added maintenance, custodial, and clerical duties to their hosting and performing commitments.

Gaining Recognition

When Mike Grilikhes became manager of the Center, he brought in Hollywood publicist Todd Faulkner to build a successful marketing strategy. With imagination and enthusiasm, Faulkner created "Celebrity Day" at the PCC. Through his airline contacts, he learned when famous people would arrive in Hawai`i.

He boarded their planes upon landing, introduced himself, and announced that the next day they would be honored at the PCC. Hotel tycoon Conrad Hilton was among the first to be recognized. With great fanfare he was whisked to the Center to enjoy "Conrad Hilton Day." These kinds of freewheeling antics probably wouldn't work in today's post-9/11 world, but it worked beautifully in 1963. Hilton was wowed, and the PCC was written up in Hilton publications around the world. Movie and television personalities were honored with their own days too, including Art Linkletter, Henry Fonda, James Garner, Tony Bennett, Johnny Mathis, Kirk Douglas, and Tony Martin, to name just a few. These luminaries of the time helped put the PCC in the media spotlight.

Government leaders were also sought out. The prime minister of Fiji, Ratu Sir Kamisese Mara, had no plans to visit Lā`ie when he came to Hawai`i. But Grilikhes changed the prime minister's mind and arranged to have him driven from Honolulu to Lā`ie with a full police escort. At the entrance, the Fijians lined up to welcome him. After giving their appropriate native greeting, they

New Zealand prime minister Sir Keith Holyoke arrives by helicopter and is greeted by a student from New Zealand. He picks up a taki, signifying that he comes in peace.

led him to the Fijian Village where the leaders from all the villages waited to greet him and participate in a carefully planned *yaqona* (kava drink ceremony). Impressed, the prime minister said that he should have come before, but was afraid he might not be happy with it.

On another occasion, the New Zealand prime minister, Sir Keith Holyoke, stopped for a brief layover in Hawai`i. The Center arranged for him to be flown from Honolulu to Lā`ie by military helicopter, which landed in the middle of the New Zealand village. According to Māori tradition, the prime minister was challenged by a warrior and then formally greeted by the village chief. Students were thrilled to meet one of their political leaders and help build goodwill for the Center.

PUBLICIZING THE PCC AT WAIKIKI

The epicenter of Hawai`i tourism is Waikiki, a magnet that attracts tens of thousands of visitors daily and where most

Elvis Presley bids farewell to the Center after filming scenes from Paradise, Hawaiian Style *there.*

Hawai`i tourist attractions maintain ticket booths. With a low promotional budget, the PCC could only afford to rent the space of one large umbrella at the International Market Place. In an overnight building project, Les Hawthorne and PCC workers constructed a small thatched hut stocked with handouts and brochures, and installed a telephone. Manned from eight in the morning until ten at night, the little hut was the Center's headquarters in Waikiki. To draw attention, personnel were on the scene to dance, sing, carve, weave, and do anything Polynesian to promote ticket sales, which gradually increased. Even today the Center maintains a presence in Waikiki, now at the Royal Hawaiian Shopping Center.

In 1966, the PCC received a boost when the king of rock and roll, Elvis Presley, filmed parts of the movie, *Paradise, Hawaiian Style,* at the Center. Mike Grilikhes negotiated a contract with Paramount Pictures, which included support for the standards of the Church. Howard Anderson monitored the agreement through the entire production in Lā`ie as well as in Hollywood where the studio segments were shot and edited.

With the release of the movie, the theme song "Drums of the Islands" (Israeli Racule's "Bula Lā`ie" with new words) soared to the top of the pop music charts. Hesitant at first to spend time outside his dressing room, Elvis gradually warmed up to the PCC workers. A farewell luau was held at the end of the filming, and Elvis climbed into his limousine with lei piled up to his ears. When an aide suggested he remove the lei for comfort during the ride, Elvis refused and wore the flowers all the way to the airport. He returned to the Center in March 1977, saying during intermission of the night show that he loved the Center and certainly planned to visit again. Unfortunately, Presley died five months later.

Faith of the Employees

Guest counts gradually improved in 1963, but it wasn't enough. By the end of the year the PCC had accumulated a net operating loss of over $61,000, and 1964 ended with an even bigger financial loss. Critics called for the Center's closure. In December 1964, as Christmas approached, a somber general manager, Les Hawthorne, called a meeting of the village coordinators: Mauga Tapusoa (Sāmoa), Joe TeNgaio (Māori), Isireli Racule (Fiji), Tehina Tapu (Tahiti), Jubilee Logan (Hawai`i), and `Emeline `Unga (Tonga). After a prayer, Hawthorne made the announcement that the Center probably wouldn't meet the next payroll because it was out of funds. There was silence as everyone absorbed the implications of the situation. But then the loyalty of the village leaders turned the meeting from despair to determination. The first to stand up was Jubilee Logan. He said, "If we cannot meet this payroll or the next one, we'll still be here. The Lord opened this place, and He is not going to close it." Mauga Tapusoa said the same thing, and every one of them stood to concur. There was not a dry eye in the room. The Center did meet its payroll that year and has done so every year since.

LEFT TO RIGHT: *Tahitian Village Chief Mapuhi; Tongan Village Chief Taumoepeau; Hawaiian Village Chief Kama; Samoan Village Chief Tufaga.*

This story illustrates a critical factor in the PCC's success, namely the heartfelt and total faith-based dedication of its employees, who have never viewed their role at the PCC as a mere job. Anchored by their goals to provide an education for their children and portray their Polynesian culture, and more especially by their rock-solid conviction that this venture was being led by God, their faith in the Center is simply unshakable. It was true in 1963 when the Center opened, and it's true today. Meli Ulayawa Lesuma, a former PCC employee, perhaps describes their feeling best: "We are all players in a Prophetic Destiny!" he said. "We know we are."[1]

Tour Companies

With his show-business background, Mike Grilikhes knew that the key to attracting large numbers of tourists was for the PCC to be included in tour packages and guidebooks. Initially the island tour companies did not include stops at the PCC, and they required commissions to do so, which the Center could not afford to pay. But as word about the PCC began to spread, more and more tourists requested visits, bringing pressure on the tour companies to add the PCC to their itineraries.

One breakthrough came when Bert Thomas, a veteran of the Hawai`i travel industry, joined the PCC as sales and marketing manager. Thomas negotiated fair commissions with several operators and set his sights on Tradewind Tours, the biggest tour company, run by his friend Bob MacGregor. Les Hawthorne claimed that the industry always followed Bob MacGregor. Hawthorne remembered the day Thomas came running into his office saying that Bob MacGregor was in the Tahitian Village. He came unannounced and stayed the entire day. He pronounced the Polynesian

Feast and the night show "great" and told Hawthorne that it had been the most enjoyable day he could remember in a long time. He claimed he wanted every tourist he brought to Hawai`i to visit the PCC and attend the night show, and when the 1966 Tradewind brochures came out, the PCC was included in seven of the nine packages. Within two years, most of the other big operators had worked out arrangements with the PCC.

Pageant of the Long Canoes

The PCC realized it needed to continually improve its attractions to gain additional visitors and attract repeat customers. Managers assessed offerings with a sharp eye to see what could be done better, a process that continues today. These efforts also helped boost the Center into the black.

Early on, David Hannemann, who was hired as the first PCC employee, recognized that tourists were not offered a chance to

A canoe filled with dancers wends its way down the lagoon.

Spectators line the banks of the lagoon for the afternoon canoe pageant.

take pictures of Polynesian dancers at the Center. Visitors at the night show were asked not to take pictures in consideration of those around them and because dancers could be momentarily blinded by the flashbulbs. Hannemann recognized the popularity of the *Kodak Hula Show* in Waikiki where tourists could shoot endless rolls of film while dancers performed in the bright sunshine. So in 1966 the canoe pageant was created to give PCC guests lots of photo opportunities. The concept was simple. Double-hulled canoes were poled down the lagoon every afternoon in a parade, with colorful costumed dancers performing on attached platforms. Each canoe represented one Polynesian culture, and the guests who lined the lagoon could snap all the pictures they wanted. From the moment the first canoe rocked down the waterway, the pageant was a great success. The *Rainbows of Paradise* has since replaced the earlier pageant and it is still a highlight of a day spent in Polynesia. Everyone wants to take pictures home.

The Promo Team

PCC performers also go on tours to promote the PCC. One of the first international tours of PCC performers took place in 1964 when sixteen students, under the direction of Jack Regas, were invited to perform in Ashiya, Japan, for a three-month gig. The Japanese sponsors replicated the Captain Cook Theater down to the last detail, including the volcano and water curtain for these performances, and the students were well received. It was a breakthrough into the lucrative Japanese tourist market.

In 1966, Hollywood entertainment mogul Sol Hurok was so impressed by the night show that he sponsored a tour for cast members. One hundred and seventy-five performers took *Festival Polynesia* on a two-week circuit that began in Los Angeles with performances at the sold-out Hollywood Bowl. Both the *Los Angeles Times* and *Newsweek* covered the event favorably. One author claimed that the performers had the Hollywood Bowl rocking like Mauna Loa during an eruption. Another praised the Samoan fireknife dance that left everyone amazed at the stunning display of skill and bravery. The cast went on to Salt Lake City, Utah, by train, where they performed six times for appreciative crowds at Highland High School auditorium.

The highlight of the students' 1966 tour to Salt Lake City was a visit with President David O. McKay, their revered prophet. He was ninety-three years old at the time and had not been to Hawai`i since he dedicated the permanent campus of the CCH in 1958. Largely through his efforts and advocacy, both the CCH and the PCC had been built. He had been their champion.

The students met briefly with President McKay in his office at the Church Administration Building in downtown Salt Lake City, and the following day they were all invited to his country home in Huntsville, Utah, for a more informal meeting where President McKay and his wife, Emma Ray, greeted the students on the front porch. It had been almost half a century since he had attended the moving flag-raising ceremony in Lā`ie and envisioned a college there. He was greatly moved that 150 Polynesian college students were on his front porch, students taking advantage of an opportunity to receive a higher education in an institution that he had founded. The visit was charged with emotion on both sides. As they were reluctantly leaving, the students sang the beautiful Samoan farewell song, President McKay's favorite, *"Tofa Mai Feleni,"* (Good-bye, My Friend). The words "Oh, I will never forget you" touched every heart. President McKay said

The Promo Team appears in Philadelphia, Pennsylvania.

Ellen Gay Dela Rosa.

he would never forget them either. He never traveled to Hawai`i again and died less than four years later in January 1970, but he had lived to see the fruits of his efforts in behalf of the Polynesian people.

When the dancers returned home to Hawai`i and their studies in September, they were welcomed by laudatory stories in the Honolulu newspapers praising their mainland performances.

Considering the enthusiastic response to these shows, PCC leaders envisioned more touring companies promoting the PCC. By 1991 this traveling group was officially referred to as the "Promo Team," and included a small group of dancers and musicians who spent their time on the road dancing at various functions. Ellen Gay Dela Rosa became the special events/ promotions team manager. In this role, Ellen Gay began training the performers in dance, as well as preparing them to speak at LDS Church firesides. She also focused on creating an atmosphere of love and respect within the troupe. The team forged a close bond. "No matter how different our backgrounds were," says performer Salamasina Tuitama, "we were still able to come together as one family."[2]

Responding to requests from alumni groups, VIP luncheons, Church firesides and more, the team continues to travel literally all over the world, thus far to five continents. They have appeared on a live broadcast of the *Today* show, danced at trade shows in Canada, performed for an audience of 30,000 in Japan on behalf of the Oahu Visitors Bureau, and attracted large audiences at Church firesides. They have danced with little sleep, and once, in Chicago, the fireknife dance had to be performed barefoot in the snow. Even though the performers continue to be amateurs, they have built a reputation of professionalism as entertainers and cultural ambassadors.

Improving the PCC

Ever investigating how the Center could be improved, PCC management helped boost guest satisfaction by rerouting the foot traffic within the Center. Originally, the front gate opened directly into the Samoan Village. Guests made a loop through the Center and went out the same gate, never passing the snack bar or gift shop. In 1965, Les Hawthorne and Emosi Damuni concluded that the entrance was in the wrong place. Without waiting for board approval, they moved the gate to a new location overnight, decorated it with two large tiki, a new sign, flowering shrubs, and a ticket office in the style of a Fijian vale. Employees coming to work the next morning found everything changed. Out-of-pocket expenses had been minimal, and the first day the snack bar did three times the business it had ever done. The gift store, Shop Polynesia (today called Mahinalani), made over one thousand dollars, four times its previous record. This success helped soothe the board's concerns that the two men had acted without approval. Employees were especially encouraged by the Shop Polynesia sales because many of the items were beautiful, authentic objects they themselves had taken great care in creating for sale in the shop. The main entrance today is near the same spot.

Hawai`i's Number One Paid Attraction

Hope began to grow that the Center was past its initial crisis and had begun to exhibit staying power. In 1967, just four years after opening, the Center registered its first profit of $208,963. President Hugh B. Brown, who had dedicated the Center five years earlier, officiated at the fifth anniversary celebration and told the workers he was gratified and amazed at the progress they had made in such a short time. David and Cynthia Eyre, editors of *Honolulu* magazine, published a story in the October 1967 issue titled, "The Flop That Flipped." In it they wrote, "The smart boys said it would never sell, but today it's one of the hottest items in Hawai`i's tourism."[3] Others praised the PCC as an improbable success and noted that it had evolved into one of Hawai`i's best known and solidly successful visitor attractions and was now an undisputed winner in one of the most fiercely competitive of all industries.

By the end of 1968, 1,132,547 guests had visited the PCC, and for the second year in a row the Center was able to give ten thousand dollars to the CCH in support of education. The high point in yearly attendance was in 1972 when 1.2 million guests visited the Center.

In 1975, more than 850,000 people visited the Lā`ie complex, half of all the tourists who visited Hawai`i that year. By that time the night show had been selling out every night for seven years. Only two free attractions in Hawai`i drew more visitors, the Honolulu Zoo and Volcanoes National Park on the island of Hawai`i. By 1977, the PCC was the top paid attraction in the islands, continuing to draw more than a million visitors a year. In 1982, the Pacific Area Travel Association presented its first Pacific Cultural Award to the PCC for doing more to preserve one or more Pacific cultures than any other organization among its thirty-nation membership.

Many factors helped move the PCC into the black. Positive publicity and recognition from tour companies certainly played their part in getting more tourists to the Center. But perhaps most important, the sacrifices and dedicated work of everyone at the PCC, students and employees alike, united and pulling together as one `ohana, moved it forward.

Former entrance to the Polynesian Cultural Center.

Much credit for the success of the PCC must also go to its sponsoring institution, The Church of Jesus Christ of Latter-day Saints, which has been unwavering in its support, providing leadership and essential financial aid at critical times, amounting to millions of dollars over the years. This financial assistance was critical in times of tourist declines in helping the PCC maintain its physical facilities. The money the Church has given, along with PCC-generated revenue and generous donations from friends, has been an investment that has generated returns many times over to support 18,000 students who have received their college educations. It has richly blessed BYU–H, which, as of 2012, has realized over $185 million in revenue from the PCC's efforts. This return on investment far exceeds the total financial support the Center has received from the Church over the years.

The PCC's success is highly dependent on the health of the Hawaiian tourist industry. This means some factors are beyond its control. In 1982, Hurricane Iwa temporarily shut down operations, and ten years later, Hurricane Iniki wreaked havoc on the state, closing the Center again.

Due to economic challenges during the Asian financial crisis of 1998, the Center restructured, and 25 percent of its full-time workforce moved into retirement. Just a few years later, the retired *kupuna* (expert teachers) began returning to work in the villages as cultural specialists, now doing as volunteers what they had been paid to do for so many years.

Perhaps the most difficult challenge began September 11, 2001, when terrorists brought down the World Trade Center in New York City. For weeks, air traffic in and out of Hawai`i was essentially shut down and only gradually resumed. Guest counts at the PCC plummeted. In an effort to help everyone retain their jobs, the Center responded not by laying people off but by reducing pay. Student paychecks stayed the same, and full-time employees and management absorbed all the cuts. Most salaries went down 10 percent, manager's salaries were reduced 20 percent, and the officers' paychecks went down 30 percent. These cuts stayed in place for two years and then were gradually raised.

Several years later, both Aloha Airlines and ATA Airlines abruptly went out of business. Thousands of tourists were stranded in Hawai`i, and the reduction in tourism necessitated a 30 percent reduction in the Center's full-time employees. Repeatedly, pay cuts went into place. From 2001 to 2010, three cycles of pay cuts were imposed, necessitated by unforeseen world events. Finally in 2011, the full-time employees received pay increases, the first time in four years. Almost unbelievably there were no complaints through any of this.

This does not mean, however, that there are no more challenges in an uncertain world. Although annual visitor counts aren't as high today as they were in the late 1960s and early 1970s, the PCC does continue to move forward, providing wonderful entertainment for tourists and critical employment opportunities for students at BYU–H and residents of Lā`ie. There is an attitude of optimism that whatever comes will be met with the same dedication, sacrifice, and hard work that have characterized the Center in the past.

Kalo Mataele Soukop, the longest serving member of the board of directors, remembers well the optimism of the early years, saying that they all knew they would be successful one day and simply wouldn't give up. Soukop had left Tonga as a young girl to attend CCH and was an original dancer at the PCC. She is now a successful businesswoman in her own right. 🌿

Chapter Eight

Foods and Feasting

At the Polynesian Feast, Howard W. Hunter, chairman of the board, and his wife, Claire (center), with their food on woven coconut platters. FAR LEFT: *Luse Tapusoa Galea`i, with T. David Hannemann* (right).

f you don't share, it doesn't taste as good." These words from a Samoan grandmother speak to the heart of the attitude about food in Polynesia, where very little happens without it. Refreshments are often the most important part of a Polynesian gathering. "When people come to your home in Hawai`i," says Cy Bridges, "the first thing you do is . . . bring them in and . . . feed them. . . . The culminating event of everything is breaking bread."[1] Fruits from backyard trees are taken to the office to share. Islanders traveling abroad carry luggage (often ice chests secured with duct tape) packed with favorite treats. It is all part of an old tradition that has survived and has ingrained itself at the PCC.

Guests enjoy the feast by sitting on woven mats on the floor, Polynesian style.

Initially PCC planners thought guests would return to Waikiki for dinner after their day at the Center, so the original Banyan Tree Snack Bar, run by concessionaires Owen and Louise Robinson, was the first and only place to buy food and drink for many years. It had a large menu for a snack bar, offering regular and teriyaki burgers, fries, fish sandwiches, salads, and custom sandwiches, and a traditional plate lunch of mahimahi curry stew. Even though it was too small almost from the beginning, the kitchen managed to outperform its small quarters.

As mentioned in chapter 7, the Banyan Tree suffered from a less-than-ideal location at first and did minimal business. When the main gate was moved in 1966, foot traffic increased and sales went up.

The Polynesian Feast

It soon became apparent that guests wanted dinner options on evenings when the night show was staged. So food services grew, like everything at the Center, from small beginnings to large and efficient operations. The first expansion came in 1964, with the debut of the Polynesian Feast, which unfolded in the Samoan chief's fale. Each village contributed one or two dishes unique to their homeland, prepared by Lā`ie families in their home kitchens and transported to the Center. The Samoans cooked their version of chop suey (still a favorite). The Māori prepared special bread, and the Tongans brought sweet potatoes and a delicious fruit drink made from crushed watermelon and pineapple. Hawaiians contributed their staple meal of poi and kālua pig hot out of the imu. The Tahitians prepared *ei ota* (raw fish salad with diced onions) and *moa fafa* (chicken with taro leaves and coconut milk). The Fijian contribution was *bulumakau rourou* (corned beef wrapped in *ti* leaves and steamed), and dessert was New Zealand trifle.

The Polynesian Feast was arrayed on six buffet tables, one for each island nation. Faannee Tapusoa, Taimi Fonoimoana, and Tauamo Malufau would spend the entire day lavishly decorating the fale with hibiscus flowers. Guests were seated on *lauhala* mats on the floor, Polynesian style, and ate from trays of woven coconut leaves called *ma`ilo*. It was an authentic island feast, and it had many elements of a luau, but it was not advertised as such. Visitors from around the world loved it and wrote glowing compliments in the guest book.

Improving Food Services

Soon after the debut of the Polynesian Feast, a new after-dinner activity was rolled out called Hauoli Sunset. Guests participated in singing, dancing, coconut husking, and drumming with Fijian derua. This authentic Polynesian experience, combined with the Polynesian Feast, provided a full evening of food and entertainment. Despite the enthusiastic response, the Polynesian Feast had to be discontinued. Food preparation was moved to the Banyan Tree kitchen to conform to government health codes that precluded cooking food for public consumption in homes. But since the Banyan Tree kitchen was just too small to service such a large undertaking, the PCC was soon stepping up to meet this new challenge.

The successful story of food services at the PCC is really the story of talented, dedicated workers who willingly put in long hours of hard work to improve their skills by special training. Emily Kaopua, a remarkable woman with the ability to duplicate any recipe from taste, was director of food and beverage services for many years. Emily began her career under the tutelage of Emily "Mom" Enos, the heart of the CCH cafeteria and the woman who fed the hungry labor missionaries during the construction of the Center in the early 1960s. Emily had studied Japanese and Chinese cuisine and had taken every food preparation course she could fit into her schedule. She even visited Disneyland and Universal Studios to observe their food operations. Emily set the bar for high standards, telling her workers, "When you prepare a sandwich, prepare it as though you were making the best sandwich for yourself."

Winona Enesa, who became the vice president of food and beverage in 1984, had worked her way up from being a bus girl and dishwasher in 1974 to leading the charge to carry on the tradition of good food service at the Center.

THE HALE KU'AI AND THE HIBISCUS BUFFET

In 1966, a new eating venue called the Hale Ku'ai was built near the Banyan Tree Snack Bar and a buffet service was offered there called the Hibiscus Buffet, in honor of the women who had so lovingly decorated the Samoan fale for the Polynesian Feast. The same menu that had been served at the Polynesian Feast was brought back, plus other American items to please the less adventurous palate. The goal was that no one would ever go away hungry or unhappy.

A year later, as lunch lines grew longer at the Banyan Tree Snack Bar, the *Komo Mai* luncheon was launched in the Hale Ku'ai. *Komo mai* in Hawaiian means "Welcome, come in." Even with the addition of the Hale Ku'ai venue, the Banyan Tree Snack Bar functioned as the main kitchen for the entire Center. For almost a decade following the opening of the Hale Ku'ai, the food service workers did the best they could in the limited facilities.

Early in 1963, an employee suggested that the hollow shells of coconuts be used to serve fruit juice during intermission at the night show. This fresh cold drink was a great hit and became the

Deelites are a favorite refreshment at the night show.

genesis of another idea, putting ice cream and pineapple chunks in a half coconut shell. Later the coconut shells were replaced with hollowed pineapple halves. Filled with pineapple chunks and topped with watermelon sherbet, the famous Deelite was born. Although use of the pineapple halves eventually had to be abandoned because they were overwhelming the available waste disposal services, the ever-popular Deelites are still served during intermission, now in plastic bowls.

As demand grew, refreshment vendors sprouted amidst the lush gardens of the Center. The first opened in 1984 in the Mission Settlement, serving cold drinks and *panipopo* (rolls baked in coconut pudding sauce). Another opened at the canoe landing near the Marquesan tohua. Since then other refreshment stands scattered among the villages have opened, selling drinks, ice cream novelties, and shaved ice.

THE MARRIOTT CONTRIBUTION

In 1977, J. Willard (Bill) Marriott, Jr., president of the worldwide hospitality giant Marriott Corporation, joined the board of directors. Marriott made a tremendous difference to food services by sharing not only his own personal knowledge of the food service business but that of other experts from his company. He invited some employees to participate in Marriott management training in Washington DC and arranged to include the PCC (and BYU–H) in Marriott purchasing and procurement arrangements to reduce costs. This agreement with Avendra, a Marriott supplier, including restaurant, kitchen, and bakery equipment, custodial supplies, and everything needed to operate a major food service facility, continues to be a great advantage to the Center.

Since 1977, either Bill Marriott, his associate Sterling D. Colton, or his brother, Richard E. (Dick) Marriott, currently chairman of the board, has been on the board of directors. The PCC has greatly benefited from such knowledge and expertise.

Carl Fonoimoana (assistant general manager for food and beverage) and Jay Akoi (purchasing) both took advantage of the Mariott management training program. Akoi's purpose was to master purchasing and procurement, but he and Fonoimoana underwent extensive training in most areas of hotel, restaurant, and hospitality management. When Akoi returned, he helped revamp the entire PCC purchasing department. Before long, Akoi and his coworkers had cut PCC costs below those of the Marriott Corporation. Fonoimoana was most interested in food service management. Other personnel, notably Emily and George Kaopua, followed them to Washington. Because of this excellent training, the food services and procurement departments were operated more economically and professionally.

The Gateway

When lines began to lengthen at the Hale Ku'ai, management cast an eye at the new orientation building. It was large, resembled a Samoan fale, and was located strategically near the Center's entrance. Already it was being used to seat overflow diners—sometimes up to four hundred people. The decision was made to renovate and dedicate the entire building to food service, and architect Steve Au redesigned a new interior to include a full-service kitchen, bakery, and dining room.

On January 12, 1979, the new Gateway opened in the old facility. A parade led by the village chiefs, a canoe pageant, and a feast helped launch the repurposed building. It was dedicated by Elder Howard W. Hunter, who was near the end of his term

as chairman of the board of directors. Customers' reactions were immediately positive. The menu and food quality were exactly the same as before, but the attractive new facility greatly improved the eating experience.

In addition to catering many sumptuous feasts for special occasions, several important internal changes in food services were launched in the 1980s. An employee lunch was introduced in 1984, adding 400 more meals a day to the demands on the kitchen. At the same time, the Center began feeding the many bus drivers who brought tourists to the Center. The kitchen was working at maximum capacity.

Max Purcell, who had experience managing large restaurants, came to the Center from Sāmoa. Like Enesa, he had held most of the jobs in the food service area before becoming manager. He pioneered the Ambassador Fine Dining (now called Prime Dining) option, also housed in the Gateway building, which appealed to the growing number of Japanese visitors. The buffet included prime rib, crab, giant shrimp, mahimahi, teriyaki, roasted chicken, and clam chowder as well as Japanese favorites such as sashime, sushi, somen, miso soup, and an enticing array of desserts, all served on tables laid with linen, silver, and candles.

The Gateway continues to evolve. In November 2011, it reopened after a complete renovation, with 24,500 square feet of space. There are thirty-eight interior columns made to look like koa logs, and the twelve-foot-high doors weigh 1,100 pounds and are carved with breadfruit and taro motifs. Guests may enjoy the Island Feast or Prime Dining in air-conditioned comfort and gaze at a 500-foot mural of King Kamehameha welcoming people from all the islands to join in the spirit of fellowship and celebration.

Luau table spread with Polynesian delicacies.

The Hale Ohana is just one of the three luau venues.

Dancers perform at the luau.

Guests are greeted at the Ali'i Luau.

The Ali'i, representing Hawaiian royalty, welcome guests to the luau.

The Luau

Right from the beginning, one thing appeared to be missing. Guests clamored for an authentic luau experience. In ancient times the luau was Hawai'i's great celebratory event. It still is. Weddings, graduations, and first-year birthdays are all celebrated with big luau, and a visit to Hawai'i simply isn't complete without experiencing one. But providing a new luau facility would require major changes, especially when most of the land at the Center was in full use. A plan was approved by the board to accommodate a new luau, and $1.3 million was budgeted for construction that started in 1994. It required rearrangement of large parts of the Center.

The first *Ali'i Luau* (chief's feast) opened in July 1996 in the former Market Place building, which had been moved from its original home behind the Hukilau Theater. On the wall of the new venue, Mataumu Alisa painted a beautiful mural of a tropical island setting to add to the décor. That project included razing the original Banyan Tree Snack Bar, which had done yeoman service since 1963. Called the Hale Ohana, the new luau venue was adequate for a few years, but demand kept growing and a second luau venue was needed.

In 2002, the old Captain Cook Theater was renovated and named the Hale Aloha to accommodate a second Ali'i Luau. The roof was extended toward the stage so diners and performers could have protection from the rain. The old stage was remodeled and enlarged at each end to accommodate the dancers and an imu. After an extensive $2.4 million renovation, the new Hale Aloha could accommodate six hundred people. Utah artist Randy Blackburn painted a new mural on the back wall of the Hale Aloha, which is the centerpiece of that venue. But it still wasn't enough for the number of guests who wanted the luau.

Several years later the Hale Ku'ai was also upgraded as a third luau venue. The PCC can now accommodate 1,350 guests at the same dinner and entertainment called the Ali'i Luau, but it is held in three different venues.

At the luau, guests are welcomed with fresh flower lei, offered ice water, photographed with young hula dancers, and led to their seats where the splash of waterfalls soothes the spirit. The haunting blowing of the conch shell announces the arrival of the Hawaiian royal court announced by attendants carrying *kahili*. The king is resplendent in traditional scarlet and gold feather cape and helmet, the queen gowned in kapa designs.

Then the dancers come on stage, performing the ancient hula kahiko. Next, the modern hula 'auana is represented by songs praising the beauty of Oahu. Dancing and music continue

Benny Kai entertains guests at the luau.

throughout dinner. Guests are encouraged to join in singing "Pearly Shells," an old favorite from the long-running radio show *Hawai`i Calls*, and the beloved island farewell song "Aloha Oe," written by the last Hawaiian monarch, Queen Liliuokalani.

The PCC offers the only luau to include *keiki* (children) dancers. The luau is also part of the most popular package tour to the PCC, which includes admission to all of the daytime activities, dinner at the Ali`i Luau, and the night show. In true Polynesian hospitality, no one goes away hungry. We let all our guests know, says Bridges, that "in Polynesia, you don't eat until you get full, you eat until you get dizzy and you're ready to pass out."[2] That is a *real* Hawaiian feast.

Food Services Continues to Evolve

The growth of the luau necessitated a new Food Processing and Distribution Center (FPDC) to prepare all food services at the Center. Nona Enesa and labor Church service missionary Dee Hunter, a specialist in food-processing facilities, in consultation with Dick Marriott, designed a state-of-the-art facility.

Requirements were demanding. It had to have a kitchen and bakery large enough to serve at least 4,000 meals a day at three major restaurants and cater to locations anywhere in the Center. It had to include sufficient storage for room-temperature dry storage as well as perishable cold-storage foods for one week, including several whole pigs ready for the nightly imu. It had to include means to move prepared hot and cold foods to various eating locations, maintaining highest quality standards. That problem was solved by portable modules that could be filled with food and pulled by electric carts to the serving areas where they were plugged in to maintain proper temperatures. In addition, it had to have a dishwasher large enough to efficiently clean enough plates, glasses, utensils, and other items for 4,000 guests and a waste disposal system that met EPA standards. And finally, it had to have a facility to launder tablecloths and napkins. It was no small order.

With architectural drawings in hand, Enesa drew the building footprint in chalk in the parking lot where it would stand and had her food workers stage a mock meal preparation. The suggestions gleaned from this exercise were incorporated into the plans. The new 16,000-square-foot, state-of-the-art FPDC, built at a cost of more than $4 million, was dedicated August 18, 1997, and met every requirement.

To please its customers, the Polynesian Cultural Center cooks 350 pounds of pork, 300 to 400 pounds of fish, 2,000 to 3,000 pounds of chicken and serves 100 pounds of poi every day. It turns out an array of salads, fresh tropical fruits, teriyaki chicken, mahi-mahi, contemporary entrées, and desserts. The number of meals produced in the FPDC every day frequently exceeds 4,000.

In March 2003, the Banyan Tree Snack Bar reopened after a $1.6 million reconstruction, still serving its popular menu prepared in its own new kitchen. The old banyan tree, which shaded the original snack bar for which it was named, had blown down, but was replaced by attractive landscaping. And now a new Banyan Tree Snack Bar is back. One innovation is that the facility is located before guests reach the PCC ticket takers, locating it outside the Center and making it available to the general public without a ticket purchase.

Fifita Unga, now head of food services, continues to emulate Emily Kaopua's philosophy of preparing each food item with love. Fifita and her staff of 35 professionals and 250 students never stop working hard to provide delicious, artistically presented meals to all who eat at the PCC. 🐝

Chapter Nine

Welcoming the World

Graduates from the joint BYU–H/PCC Asian Executive Management Training Program.

The PCC is a magnet for people all over the world. Besides the daily attendance, it usually hosts about one thousand dignitaries from fifty to seventy-five different countries each year. "Here is this little tiny town on this little island in the middle of this gigantic ocean, and it is exercising an influence around the world that is incredible,"[1] said Von Orgill.

The China Connection

The Center shares a unique relationship with the People's Republic of China. Such a thing seemed remote when the Center opened in 1963, because the United States and China did not then have diplomatic relations. Few Americans visited China and few Chinese visited the United States, certainly not as tourists. But when formal diplomatic relations were restored between the two countries on January 1, 1979, the doors opened. That summer the Young Ambassadors, a student performing group from BYU–Provo, were well received when they toured China, and other groups followed. BYU campuses, both Provo and Hawai`i, became as well known in China as the Ivy League schools.

Asian Executive Management Training Program

In 1980, China's vice premier, Geng Biao, and fourteen Chinese generals visited the United States. Surprisingly, at the last minute, they requested a stop in Hawai`i to tour the Polynesian Cultural Center. The US Secret Service and military scrambled to make the necessary arrangements.

Geng Biao was so impressed with the Center that he immediately began talking about building a similar place in China to highlight his country's rich cultural heritage. Bill Cravens, then PCC general manager, suggested instead that China send their own people to Lā`ie to learn how to build and operate a center for themselves. Students could attend BYU–H on student visas and work at the PCC for firsthand experience and training. Geng Biao was immediately interested and agreed to the arrangement on the spot. Elliot Cameron, then president of BYU–H, joined the group, carrying a stack of admission applications. By the time the meeting ended, a unique and mutually beneficial cultural exchange had been organized.

The program began almost immediately with the arrival and enrollment in September 1981 of six Chinese students, one of whom had been an interpreter traveling with Geng Biao's party. These were midlevel executives and scholars, not young college students, and their tuition was paid by the Chinese government. In 1985, the program was formalized with the name Asian Executive Management Training Program. Every year, until the difficulties caused by the terrorist attacks on 9/11, as many as fourteen Chinese men and women—able executives who work in the travel, hotel, and restaurant industries, as well as in provincial foreign affairs offices in China—have been selected by their leaders to enter the program. By 2011, 211 had completed it. To qualify, they must first exhibit proficiency in English. Once enrolled at BYU–H, they take twelve credits each semester, for two semesters, including a religion class. Their courses of study are designed to give them experiences to enhance their own careers. At the completion of the ten-month program they receive a certificate of completion from both PCC and BYU–H. Virtually all interns in the program have been promoted immediately upon their return home to China and have risen as leaders in their companies and government assignments. They now constitute an enthusiastic alumni group who eagerly gather when PCC and BYU–H representatives visit China.

Visits of Chinese Dignitaries

In January 1984, PCC leaders were thrilled when they learned from President Gordon B. Hinckley, that Premier Zhao Ziyang, China's top leader, had requested through the White House a visit to the PCC on his way to Washington DC to meet with US President Ronald Reagan. Premier Zhao's large entourage included a delegation of forty-six leaders.

Newly appointed president and general manager of the Center, Ralph G. Rodgers, with help from BYU–H, arranged for the visit. The premier wanted to see the whole Center, including the villages. This request alone required hours of planning by Secret Service personnel as they worked out the safest routes. The lagoon and all the bridges needed to be checked to be sure no explosive devices were hidden there.

Premier Zhao arrived by US Marine helicopter on the grounds in front of the McKay Special Events building on the BYU–H

campus. Elder Marvin J. Ashton, then chairman of the board of directors of the PCC, and his wife, Norma, and Ralph Rodgers and Elliot Cameron and their wives greeted the premier with beautiful lei. He was impressed by the warmth and genuine personal interest of the greetings he received. He was shown around the villages, and attended a special morning performance of the night show *This is Polynesia*. At the luncheon afterward, BYU–H students representing twenty nations served the premier and his group. Many of the Chinese delegates asked questions about the university, the PCC, and about life in America.

Elliot Cameron noted that the visit to the PCC was the only cultural event planned during the premier's entire visit to the United States, and it was the single longest activity on the delegation's itinerary. They wondered why the premier had singled out

Chinese premier Zhao Ziyang (center, seated) *visits the Center in 1984. Elder Marvin J. Ashton is on the left.*

the PCC, but it would be almost a year and a half before that mystery was solved.

Among the first six students to come to Lāʻie as part of the Asian Executive Management Training Program was a young woman named Wang Yannan. She had worked at the PCC like other students and attended classes at BYU–H. In June 1983, she received an associate of arts degree magna cum laude in hotel and travel management. No one knew until graduation that she was Premier Zhao's daughter. She never revealed her secret during the two years she was in Lāʻie, but her glowing reports of life at the PCC and BYU–H obviously stirred the premier's curiosity. He had to see the PCC for himself.

Other important Chinese national and provincial leaders visited the Center. In 1994, 162 Chinese dignitaries came to see for themselves too, including Vice Premier Zou Jiahua, mayors, ministers of various national industries, leaders of cultural groups, and performers.

Proving the old adage that imitation is the highest form of flattery, many foreign visitors dream of replicating the Center in their own countries. Les Moore (PCC president 1991–2000) said that during his tenure he received over seventy requests for help to replicate the PCC. "Because they felt the spirit," said Les, "they wanted it!"[2] China was one country that followed through.

Ma Chi Man was head of the China Travel Service and was often called the "Walt Disney of China." Ma's daughter Shirley (Shellen) Ma also attended BYU–H and became a foreign tour guide for the PCC, leading both Mandarin and English tours. Ma himself was fascinated by the PCC, and he became an advocate for creating a cultural showcase in China patterned after the Center. When he visited Lāʻie, he inspected everything and learned about operations and offerings in detail. Ma's efforts eventually resulted in a Chinese cultural center in Shenzhen, China.

The China Folk Culture Villages

The China Folk Culture Villages became a reality in 1991. David Hannemann and Reg Schwenke, PCC vice president, represented the Center at the grand opening, which proved to be a cultural feast beyond compare. To convey their roles as cultural ambassadors, Hannemann and Schwenke went barefoot and wore formal lavalava with the bright red-and-yellow shirts of the PCC Samoan Village. Around their necks were Fijian salusalu, and in their hands they carried fine Polynesian-carved walking sticks. They attracted considerable attention as they walked the streets of the new facility and participated in the parades, dinners, and other festivities. Everyone wanted pictures taken with them.

The twenty-four villages of the Chinese center represent distinct cultures chosen from among the fifty-six minorities found in mainland China, one of the world's oldest and most sophisticated cultures. The grand and elegant Chinese center was meticulously constructed. They invested more than $30 million in the project, almost thirty times the budget originally expended on the PCC. The China Folk Culture Village is a generous gift to the Chinese people and the world, and the PCC representatives were grateful that their own Center had been the inspiration.

Sister Cultural Centers

This association led Ma to suggest an agreement between the PCC and the China Folk Culture Villages to become sister cultural centers. The PCC, with 1,200 employees living on an island with fewer than a million people, was invited to join hands with a Chinese cultural center owned by the China Travel Service, an organization with over 14,000 employees, in a country of over a billion people. The PCC board of directors was flattered that the China Travel Service would seek such an arrangement, and after review by the legal team, the offer was enthusiastically accepted.

In May 1992, seven months after the grand opening in China, Lester W. B. Moore, newly appointed president and general manager of the PCC, and David Hannemann visited China to hold serious discussions toward a reciprocal agreement. They were pleased to learn of the credibility and respect that the PCC holds in the eyes of experts and owners of cultural theme parks. The Chinese made it clear that they regard the PCC as the world leader and model of excellence to aspire to and pattern themselves after. Considering the remarkable quality of the theme parks in Shenzhen alone (other culture villages have since been constructed in China), the PCC could not have been more highly complimented.

In August 1992, Ma Chi Man arrived in Lā`ie for the formal signing of the "Memorandum of Understanding" that bound the PCC and the China Folk Culture Villages as sister institutions. The agreement provides for the sharing of information regarding cultural presentations, exhibits, and demonstrations; for exchanges of promotional entertainment of individuals, teams, and groups; and for cooperation for the mutual benefit of both institutions. After the signing, a lavish banquet was served and a grand celebration followed with every village presenting its best gifts to the Chinese visitors complemented by spectacular singing and dancing. This mutually beneficial agreement still remains in effect.

In May 1996, another significant event occurred when President Gordon B. Hinckley, his wife, Marjorie, and a party of Church leaders visited the China Folk Culture Villages after dedicating the first LDS temple in Hong Kong. President Hinckley had toured China in 1980 as an Apostle, but this was his first visit since becoming President of the Church. He was given the red carpet treatment by the Chinese (a red carpet was literally rolled out), who identified him throughout the visit as the "President of the Polynesian Cultural Center," (not as president of the entire Church), showing their admiration for the Center.

Continued Association with China

Chinese visitors kept coming to the PCC. In the fall of 1994, Les Moore was asked to host another leader from China, Vice Premier Li Lanqing. Vice Premier Li was responsible for all cultural and religious affairs in China and was on his way to Washington DC to meet with US president Bill Clinton for the purpose of signing a $1.2 billion dollar trade agreement between the United States and the People's Republic of China. The visit to the PCC was planned for November 12.

Les Moore remembered that Elder Russell M. Nelson, who had responsibility for China as a member of the Quorum of the Twelve, was scheduled to be in Honolulu that same week. As a physician, Elder Nelson had performed open heart surgery on many prominent Chinese people in China and held honorary degrees at Chinese universities. Elder Nelson's itinerary had him leaving Hawai`i at noon the next day, but learning of this opportunity to meet with the vice premier, he rescheduled his flight and made plans to be at the PCC.

At the PCC, Elder Nelson greeted Vice Premier Li in his own language. The vice premier, visibly impressed and in perfect English, responded, "Dr. Nelson, you're Chinese. Come sit by me." Elder Nelson and the vice premier were together for the next six hours. The warm relationship they developed at the

PCC performers were invited to the ceremonies in 2000 at the handover of Hong Kong to China.

PCC led to another meeting in February of 1995 at the Summer Palace in China with Li Lanqing, Elder Nelson, Elder Neal A. Maxwell, and Elder Kwok Yuen Tai, then president of the Asia Area for the Church.

An unimaginable amount of planning on the part of many PCC employees took place to make each of these visits successful. Motorcades had to be organized, flower and fruit baskets delivered to hotel rooms, breakfast, lunch, and dinner menus prepared, and food served. Special singing and dancing performances were scheduled, all this as the normal work at the PCC continued. The effort and cost of these visits was substantial, but no one complained. They knew their efforts would have positive long-term results toward establishing good relationships between the People's Republic of China and the Church, and they were pleased to do their part.

THE BLESSING OF HONG KONG

On July 1, 1997, control of Hong Kong was turned over to the People's Republic of China after ninety-nine years of British rule. Elder Kwok Yuen Tai invited the Polynesian Cultural Center to send a performance team to participate in the massive parade (over seventy groups) and other festivities that would accompany the handover.

The Promo Team made preparations to join the turnover celebration in Hong Kong. John Muaina, PCC vice president for human resources, led the group of thirty performers. In Hong Kong, they met with about thirty Chinese students at the LDS institute of religion there. The two groups became immediate good friends as the PCC performers taught their new Chinese friends to do Tongan and Samoan dances.

Parade day arrived with extremely heavy rain, not unusual in Hong Kong. Not discouraged, the Promo Team left their hotel for the parade. But the rains continued as the three buses carrying the students wound through Hong Kong's narrow streets. At the beginning of the parade route, they found things strangely quiet. Soon they learned that the parade had been cancelled, though they had not been notified. They were unsure what to do next.

Muaina suggested they pray, and they knelt as best they could in the crowded aisles. He recalled saying, "Lord, we are all here as you requested. We don't understand the events of this morning and we know, however, that thou would do with us as thy will would be done . . . and we will follow your will." Quietly they all echoed "Amen." Ten minutes passed as they waited for an answer. Then the event organizer bounded onto the bus. "I have good news," he said. "You won't believe this. . . . They want us to perform on national TV!" The students erupted in loud cheers as they laughed and cried and hugged each other in astonishment.

"Our kids dressed up, went out . . . into a large stadium," said John, "where there was only us, . . . the only group that was going to perform on national TV and they apologized for that! And our kids stood in front with their banner that said 'Brigham Young University–Hawai`i Campus—Polynesian Cultural Center,' all written in Mandarin and our audience was over 100 million people. . . . We had international news press there and we were the only ones that they could interview. We were the only ones they could take pictures of." John concluded, "[We] knew that the hand of the Lord was in that event and we had no control over it. All we had to do was follow."[3] 🦑

Chapter Ten

Our Hearts Become One

LĀʿIE HAWAII TEMPLE

BYU—HAWAIʿI

POLYNESIAN CULTURAL CENTER

Aerial view of Lāʿie showing the three major institutions that constitute what President Howard W. Hunter called the Triad of Learning.

I n 1994, President Howard W. Hunter referred to the three institutions in Lā`ie—the temple, the Polynesian Cultural Center, and Brigham Young University–Hawai`i—as the "Triad of Learning," and said that they had a significant place in the plan of the Lord to further the work of His kingdom. President Gordon B. Hinckley commented on the same thing in 2003. "We have here something that we have nowhere else in all the world," he said. " . . . [Lā`ie] becomes one great and beautiful and magnificent campus."[1]

The founding of the Polynesian Cultural Center in 1963 as a separate institution increased BYU–H's ability to educate its students by providing critical financial support. Without the college there might not have been the need or motivation to establish the PCC. But without the PCC, BYU–H could not have filled its mission to educate large numbers of Polynesians and students from around the world. Both institutions have unique roles in the same endeavor and share a symbiotic relationship. They are, as Eric Shumway, former president of BYU–H and acting president of the PCC, observed, "joined at the heart."[2]

The Triad of Learning is more than three institutions and a collection of buildings in a small country town. It is a dynamic that involves the minds, hearts, and efforts of the whole community working together to create an imperfect but special place where every day the Spirit is felt and hearts are touched. The management, full-time employees, students, and volunteers at the PCC; the administration, faculty, and staff of BYU–H; those who keep the temple operating; and the people of Lā`ie continue to be guided by their common belief and dedication to the gospel of

Jesus Christ. Visitors to the PCC feel this collective spirit. They don't always know exactly how to describe it, but they say it is warm and wonderful, and they wish they could find some way to hold on to it, package it in a bottle, and take it home.

This spirit was evident early on. At the second commencement exercises, President Reuben Law was asked for a breakdown of the CCH student body by country of origin. He responded with a partial list: Hawaiians and part-Hawaiians, 140; Caucasians, 68; Japanese, 29; Chinese, 19; Philippinos, 19; Samoans, 16. "I almost hesitate to mention this breakdown because here in Hawai`i, regardless of race, we are one united family of people."[3]

"If you live the gospel [of Jesus Christ]," said Shumway, "which is a gospel of love, a gospel of patience, flexibility, a gospel of truth, a gospel of mercy . . . you will discover that all cultural barriers fall."[4] When that happens, your life will be enriched, the lives of those around you will be enriched, and your community will be prepared to become a beacon light to the world that will come seeking to know what is different about your community. Lā`ie, the most culturally diverse place in Hawai`i, is an example of this process.

Becoming one doesn't mean to "subsume your own culture," explains BYU–H professor Debbie Hippolite Wright. "[You continue to] live it, appreciate it. But [you also learn] to appreciate the similarities and differences of other people's cultures."[5]

Cy Bridges put it this way: "The gospel brings . . . us together, and we become one, one in heart, one in mind, one in goal. We believe the same things, we hope the same things, we strive and strengthen one another towards the same goals. And in essence then our cultures become one. . . . Our hearts speak the same language."[6]

In 1973, President Marion G. Romney, counselor in the First Presidency of the Church, observed that, "[Lā`ie] is a living laboratory in which individuals who share the teachings of the master teacher have an opportunity to develop an appreciation, tolerance, and esteem for one another. For what can be done here inter-culturally in a small way is what mankind must do on a large scale, if we are ever to have real brotherhood on this earth."[7]

The PCC offers a thriving example of how people from many cultures can interact in harmony by applying the Christian values of loving your brother or sister as yourself. It is the highest manifestation of the famous Hawaiian spirit of aloha, or love, proving that Christianity works.

Intercultural tolerance, respect, and understanding do not happen by chance. They come through valuing and working at tolerance, empathy, respect, appreciation, and learning from failures. The PCC has been fortunate to have management teams who have exemplified this unity. Over the years, managers have come from the US mainland, many island nations, Australia, and elsewhere. They have been strong leaders who lead with love and resolve problems and differences with charity, always striving to build a consensus that recognized each other's concerns and everyone's effort.

The Students

The students make up 60 to 70 percent of the employee population at the Center. Through demonstrations and performances they become living examples of their own cultures. But they do much more than that. They learn to appreciate and value other cultures as they interact with each other. Because students are the main interface with guests, they have the opportunity to pass this spirit to hundreds of thousands of visitors every year, communicating a warmth, friendliness, kindness, hospitality, and love rarely seen or experienced in other places.

Daniel Ng, a student from Singapore, described it. He said he had come to understand that aloha involved much more than saying hello and good-bye. "I think . . . it involves a spirit of reaching out and bringing people into your family. Like treating one another as real brothers and sisters. . . . That's the spirit I felt when I came [to Lā`ie]."[8] Lā`ie, the ancient city of refuge, became a gathering place for Hawaiians in 1865, and today it is a place of refuge and gathering place for the world.

The Employees

Many individuals, families, and generations of families have been associated with the PCC for decades, providing a reservoir of great depth, strength, and wisdom. These employees have given their hearts to the cause. On his first day as president of the Center, Les Moore added up the combined years of experience of his new colleagues. "There was something like 500 years of experience," he remarked. He knew the Center was in good hands. When you bring that kind of "spirituality, intelligence, and experience . . . together and focus it, [you can] solve any problem," he added.[9]

The full-time employees also provide a great service to the student employees who are far away from home, as they lovingly act as surrogate parents. Because of long distances, lack of money, and the need for jobs at the Center to continue year round, most Polynesian students leave their homes for college and rarely return home until they have completed their studies. Employees at the Center fill their need for family with love, advice, and acceptance, providing a true anchor.

Ivin and Pearl Gee from Lander, Wyoming, were the first senior missionaries to serve at the Center.

The Service Missionaries

A third group of people makes the PCC an exceptional place. In November 1984, Ivin and Pearl Gee from Lander, Wyoming, were the first senior missionaries to serve at the Center. Since then a small army of LDS Church members have come as service or senior missionaries. After 9/11, with its resulting financial challenges, the number of senior missionaries increased to as many as forty-eight at a time. Adding even more strength is an average of twenty-eight local volunteers who also donate time at the Center. Senior couples pay their own way and serve wherever they are needed, usually for eighteen months. If the Center needs carpenters, electricians, or plumbers, service missionaries are called to fill the need. They've helped with marketing, computer programming, information systems, and networks, and willingly do anything that is needed. "We estimate conservatively that the [service] missionaries save the Center about $2 million a year,"[10] says Von Orgill.

The Community

PCC also reaches out to the local community to share its spirit, hosting dozens of events during the year. One of the best known is the World Fireknife Championships, called the "world's hottest event," which has been held for almost twenty years with competitors coming from all over the world. Other annual events include the Moanikeala Hula Festival, and the *Whakataetae*, a Māori song and dance competition that annually attracts almost two thousand competitors. Annual May Day celebrations for nearby elementary schools are held each year in the Pacific Theater, and concerts and lectures are open to the public. The

As a good neighbor, the PCC hosts many competitions,
exhibitions, and festivals during the year.

20 YEARS
WORLD FIREKNIFE Championships
MAY 9-12, 2012

DATE MAY 12, 2012

FOUR THOUSAND DOLLARS $ 4,000.00

PAY

TO THE ORDER OF   JOSEPH CADOUSTEAU

Center awards district and Hawai'i state Teacher of the Year awards, presents five-hundred-dollar scholarships to deserving high school seniors every spring, and hosts an annual arts festival. In many significant ways, the PCC is a good neighbor. As part of

its community outreach, the PCC issues discount tickets for local school children to come to the Center on field trips, and more than twenty thousand children a year do so.

So much about the PCC is the opposite from what most people expected. Its location, far away from the Waikiki center of tourism was seen as a detriment, but it turns out that's what tourists wanted—to get away from the Waikiki atmosphere and experience a little of true Polynesia. Critics said tourists would never pay to see students sing and dance, but they were wrong there too. The enthusiastic amateur performers have proven to be more attractive to tourists than professionals. Some said (perhaps correctly) that the Polynesian cultures were fading under the assault of modern Western influences, but those traditions are lovingly preserved at the PCC. Students thought they were coming to Lā'ie for an education, but they gain a prize of equal value as they learn to love people from all over the world.

In 2013 the PCC will celebrate its fiftieth anniversary. The PCC 'ohana looks forward to the next fifty years with great optimism. Von Orgill spoke for all of them when he said, "I fully anticipate that our greatest days are yet ahead. I think marvelous things have occurred at the Center in the past. And yet, as we look forward, I believe we will see and experience things that will amaze us in a myriad of wonderful ways. . . . There are real ways we can be even more of a living museum, a living classroom portraying the best of Polynesia. And, as we work at bringing the past, present and future generations more closely together, we will have a wonderful impact on guests and employees alike. By reaching into the spirit of yesteryear and by expanding the vision for the future . . . [we can all] join . . . to build on what the Center has already become . . . Polynesia's showcase"[11] and a community bonded in love. 🌿

Acknowledgments

There are literally hundreds of people who have contributed to this book, and though it would be impossible to mention most of them by name, my gratitude to each one is enormous.

By the time I was asked to write this history, the project had already gone through several drafts. Even though I started anew, I am indebted to R. Lanier Britsch, Rita Ariyoshi, and Lee Cantwell, who produced their own versions of the history. I am especially indebted to Lanier Britsch, whose scholarly histories of Polynesia and Hawai`i, listed in the bibliography, have for many years been the definitive works in this area.

All the people at the Polynesian Cultural Center have been anxious to have this history written and have given much time and effort to see it happen. I have greatly benefited from their strength, wisdom, and generosity. I am grateful to Von Orgill, Alfred Grace, Wilda Paalua, and the whole PCC `ohana—a true family of past and present employees, students, board members, and volunteers—for their generous sharing of stories, warm hospitality, interviews, and answers to questions. Bobby Akoi and David Hannemann made a heroic effort to identify the images. No matter what I asked of them, they always came through. Their love for the Center and their continuing sacrifices to make it so successful have in turn inspired my best efforts.

Also my warmest thanks to Jana Erickson, Leslie Stitt, Richard Erickson, and Tonya Facemyer and all the people at Deseret Book for their expertise, and to Dave Cole, Ty Jeppesen, Curtis Barlow, and their colleagues at Design Farm for their inspired work. Without their professional attention this would still be a manuscript on the shelf.

My grateful thanks also to David Hannemann and his wife, Carolyn. David has been the father of this project, and for well over a decade he has worked tirelessly to bring it to fruition. As the first full-time employee at the Center, he lived most of its history while making major contributions to its success. Now serving as the historian, he has amassed a large archive to preserve that history, which he generously made available to me. His kindness and support as a collaborator were invaluable.

My thanks, too, for the never-failing interest and support of my wonderful family, and especially my husband, Mark. He insisted that this story had to be told. He was my first reader, and the manuscript bears many evidences of his insights and wise suggestions. Our shared love of Hawai`i and of the Polynesian Cultural Center and his willingness to be a ready advisor every step of the way made it seem like a joint project. It would be true to say that without him and his contributions the book could not have been completed. 🌿

Appendix A—Labor Missionaries

Labor missionaries who constructed the PCC 1960–1963

Cook Islands
Ngatikaura, Teinakore

Hawai`i
Alo, Uga and Savii
Broad, Gordon
Cabrera, Archie
Ekau, Herman Naleiaha
Fa`aloga, Taualii
Fely, Vaitogi
Garrigan, James and Mabel Ponoui
Haiku, Antone Jr. and Agnes Leialoha Aniu
Hao, Earl
Hose, Norman
Huber, Walter and Elma Ann
Inere, LeRoy Cornelio
Kaaihue, George
Kahoohanehano, Oliver
Kalohilani, Wallace
Kamae, Jr., Henry E. L.
Kanahele Jr., William
Kapeliela, George
Kapu, Samuel
Kapu III, John
Keawe, John and Emalia
Kekauoha, William Waa (Pumpkin)
Keliliki, Dale
Keuma, Wilton
Koahou, Fuatino Su`a

Koula, Fisilau
Kumukoa, Joe
Kupihea, George
Kupihea, Roy
Leatutufu, Siitia Laita and Saluvale
Leota, Fa`aolaataga Tapuvae
Logan, Jubilee Maiola and Eugenia K.
Low, Dallas D.
Low, Mark K.
Magalei, Solomona
Makahi, Nonaina H.
Nahinu, Charles
Nahinu, Samuel
Namauu, Gladiol
Ohumukini, Itasco and Elsie
Oshima, Eugene
Po`uha, Nafetalia Rfeki and Velesenelia
Russell, Marcel Albert Sr. and Rose Loki
Salima, Feleti T.
Savaiigea, Talai Fili
Spencer, Orlando
Tanimoto, Lloyd
Uale, James A. and Elizabeth Crichton
Waiwaiole, Samuel

New Zealand
Apiti, Hohepa D.
Archibald, James
Edwards, Sam
Elkington, John A. and Waitohi
Elkington, Wahanui Tupaea
Hirini, Bob
Mason, William Newell
McCarthy, Derek

McKay, Oliphant
Mihaere, Rufus
Murray, Thomas
Neyemihyer, Rufus
Ngawaka, Tehata Robert
Panere, Taka
Paracana, Nepia
Rarere, Karepa John
Tahau, Nana
TeHira, Percy
TeNgaio, Joseph and Millie
Wihongi Jr., Rika

Niue Islands
Poluhua, Nafetelai Feki and Velesenelia

Sāmoa
Afuvai, Mulia`au
Alo, Uga and Savaii
Alofipo, Kalisi
E`etau, Tupu Vaega`au
Feleti, Fuiava Fa`aaliga
Gasu, Mata`ese
Lameko, Lita
La`ulu, Tuvae T.
Leatutufu, Laita and Saluvate
Manu, Sekeli Sale
Mauga, Apete
Maui`a, Hitler
Nautu, Sauaina
Papalii, Leagaoletaua Harold
Pei, Soloa
Sagapolu, Toa`itiiti Moevasa
Soifua, Vaeoletalalelei M.

Solo`ai, Sakaria
Soloni, Fa`atali Laupola
Su`a, Tumena
Tafau, Palati
Tanielu, Popo
Te`o, Matina Leti
Toelupe, Lafi
Tofa, Alapati Penu`ofa
Togia, Pouvi Tagatauli

Tonga
Alusa, Nafetalai
Brown, Semisi Kalanite, Talana S.
Fatani, David Lupeituu and Loto Langi
Feinga, Sione
Fevaleaki, Ma`ake Sami and Mele
Finau, Siosiua Polotini and Meleane S.
Folau, Tonga Mohenoa and Laina Vea
Kaufusi, Henry Vea
Kauvaka, Likitoni
Langi, Afe Uoleva and Ana Finau
Latu, Hingano H.
Lavaka, Tevita T.
Lomu, Mosese Lusia
Lutui, Vaikalafi and Mele Vavasa
Mafi, Nuku M.
Mapa, Hiliate
Mata`ele, Kalolaine Soukop
Mohenoa, Tonga and Laina Vea
Mohetau, David Ma`ukakala
Olive, Heamasi Kaulave and Naina
Olive, Semisi Mo`unga
Polotini, Siosilua and Meleane
Pulotu, Sione Tuione

Pututau, Sione Siliku and Sioana
Samani, Fatafehi
Sami, Ma`ake and Mele
Soifua, Vaeloetalalelei M.
Sulunga, Sione Feongoi
Toki, Solomon Tupou
Tuione, Kelikupa A.K.
Tuiono, Po`asi
Tupou, Lualala Akolea
Tupou, Tevita Akolea and Lesieli
`Unga, Pita Afu and `Emeline
Valikoula, Fisilau
Vea, Ika Moana
Vea, Simote Liloi and Ana Saulala
Vehekite, Kite Tuita

Unknown
Ekau, Herman Naleiaha
Tumanacore, Paul E.
Owius, Ole

USA—Mainland
Andersen, Horace and Anna
Andrews, Joseph

Barton, Ray and Luella
Boe, Arnold and Ann Wilson
Boe, Harold and Sylvia
Bowden, Clarence
Bowers, Lewis Christian and Clothiel C.
Bowles, George A. and Vivian M.
Buck, Joseph Samuel and Etna Wheeler
Burkhead, Major Benton and Genevieve
Butcher, Duane H. and Valene C.
Cheney, Alton and Hildegard
Combs, Jack D. and Carma R.
Cottle, J. Archie and Mildred
Dahle, Alton Hill and Zelda
Day, L. Movell and Helen
Dennis, Rex Howard and Phyllis
Devereaux, Norman and Ruth
Ferrin, Marvin J. and Delila
Guerts, Theodore I. (Ted) and Fay
Hailstone, Morgan L. and Mamie
Hales, Melvin D. and Nondas
Hansen, Anthony T. and Blanche
Harris, Grant and Ann
Hathaway, Anthony F. and Elina
Hegman, LaDell

Horrell, Douglas
Horrell, Michael
Hughey, Ralph
Hurst, John E. and Bertha R.
Jarman, Vernon and Ethel
Jasperson, Glade L. and Elma
Johnson, G. Cecil and Eleatha
Johnson, Erick I. and Esther
Johnson, Emil W. and Lisa
Kleinman, David Conrad and Ellen Jane
Knight, Joseph B.
Larson, Carl G. and Selma
Lynn, Fred M. and Viola
Maxfield, LuDean and Ella
Manwaring, Lavell and Ivy G.
Martindale, Alvin and Alice
Nielsen, Donald R. and Dixie Lee
Norton, Joseph J. and Mildred
Nielsen, J. Wells and Virginia D.
Oliphant, Arden and Lucille
Olson, Alma A. and Huldah
Pack, Paul M. and Alice C.
Pierce, John J. Jr. and Ilene
Protzman, Paul L. and Maxine

Ridd, Heber E. and Etta Day
Robinson, Owen B. and Louise
Stevens, Woodrow W. and Pearl
Schneider, Miles R. and Stella
Short, Derek Grant and Connie
Stoker, Leslie W. and Annie W. Stoker
Swickard, Ronald Gordon and Merrilee
Terry, George C. and Jessie
Thompson, Christian Roy and Lola
Thompson, Heber C. and Mary Louise
Tucker, Andrew C. and Hannah
Trump, Charles A. and Eva
Tyler, Joseph and Bernice
Tyler, Virginia
Venema, Albert and Loveina
Wall, George M.
Waterman, Albert Clark and Leota
Wheat, Hosea L. and Hattie
Wilson, Gene and Alena Wilson
Wilson, Joseph and Pearl
Wilson, Robert L. and Luella
Wilson, Wilbur J. and Marilyn
Wolfgramm, Charles A. and Verna M.
Yancey, John D. and Arlene

Appendix B—Leadership

Chairmen of the Board of Directors of the PCC

Wendell B. Mendenhall
August 1963–January 1965

Howard W. Hunter
January 1965–April 1976

Marvin J. Ashton
April 1976–July 1988

Dallin H. Oaks
January 1987–September 1996

Joseph B. Wirthlin
January 1987–September 1996 (vice chairman)

Theodore M. Jacobsen
January 1993–February 2005

Mark H. Willes
February 2005–October 2009

Richard E. Marriott, Jr.
October 2009–present

General Managers/Presidents/ Managing Directors of the PCC

Howard B. Stone
August 1963–December 1963

Edward L. Clissold
January 1964–August 1964 (acting)

Rad B. Robinson
May 1964–August 1964 (acting)

Michel M. Grilikhes
August 1964–October 1964

Lester C. Hawthorne
October 1964–November 1964

F. Wayne Glaus
January 1966–October 1967

Lawrence Haneberg
October 1967–August 1968

George Q. Cannon
August 1968–March 1975 (acting)

William H. Cravens
March 1975–April 1983

Ralph G. Rodgers
April 1983–July 1988

James P. Christensen
July 1988–June 1991

Eric B. Shumway
June 1991–October 1991 (acting)

Lester W. B. Moore
October 1991–June 2000

Von D. Orgill
June 2000–Present

Members PCC Board of Directors–1963–2012

Edward LaVaun Clissold, August 1963–April 1976
George Q. Cannon, August 1963–January 1992
Owen J. Cook, August 1963–November 1971
D'Monte Combs, August 1963–January 1965
John A. Elkington, August 1963–January 1965
Kenneth Farrer, August 1963–January 1965
Michel M. Grilikhes, September 1963–September 1965
Lawrence Haneberg, August 1963–April 1976
Gus Tafu Hannemann IV, August 1963–April 1965
William K. Isaass, August 1963–April 1965
Clinton J. Kanahele, August 1963–April 1965
Jerry K. Loveland, August 1963–January 1965
D. Lawrence McKay, August 1963–November 1976
Wendell B. Mendenhall, August 1963–April 1976
Max W. Moody, August 1963–January 1965
Ralph D. Olsen, August 1963–January 1965
George W. Poulsen, Jr., August 1963–January 1965
Howard B. Stone, August 1963–September 1964
Paul Su`afilo, August 1963–January 1965
Joseph E. Wilson, August 1963–January 1965
Charles A. Wolfgramm, August 1963–January 1965
Richard D. Wootton, August 1963–January 1964
Howard B. Anderson, March 1964–April 1976
Harry V. Brooks, March 1964–January 1965
F. William Gay, March 1964–October 1994
Rad B. Robinson, March 1964–January 1965
Joseph R. Smith, March 1964–September 1964
T. Bowring Woodbury, May 1964–January 1965
Howard W. Hunter, January 1965–April 1976
Stephen L. Bower, November 1971–July 1974
Dan W. Anderson, October 1974–July 1980
Marvin J. Ashton, April 1976–July 1988
Faasea Mailo, April 1976–July 1977
Ralph G. Rodgers Jr., January 1977–May 1988
J. Willard Marriott Jr., April 1977–May 1988
Fred A. Baker, September 1978–June 1994
Ben E. Lewis, September 1978–July 1979
Jeffrey R. Holland, October 1979–October 1990
D. Arthur Haycock, April 1986–September 1989

Dallin H. Oaks, January 1987–June 1996
Joseph B. Wirthlin, July 1988–June 1996
Sterling D. Colton, November 1988–January 1995
Herbert K. Sproat, January 1990–October 1990
John A. Hoag, June 1990–October 1993
Dee F. Anderson, June 1991–October 1999
Eric B. Shumway, January 1992–February 2005
Kalolaine Mata`ele Soukop, January 1992–present
Theodore M. Jacobsen, January 1993–February 2005
Boyd K. Mossman, June 1994–present
Richard E. Marriott, June 1995–present
W. Allen Doane, June 1995–July 1999
D. Lloyd Hunter, June 1996–June 2001
John P. Monahan, June 1996–present
Alton L. Wade, June 1996–March 2000
Mark H. Willes, June 1996–October 2009
Brad W. Farnsworth, July 1996–February 2006
V. Napua Baker, July 2000–October 2009
Albert Y. G. Ho, July 2000–December 2003
James R. Long, July 2000–present
Ira A. Fulton, October 2003–present
Daniel P. Howells, June 2006–present
J. Chris Lansing, June 2006–present
Donald L. Staheli, June 2006–October 2008
Jackie B. Trujillo, June 2006–present
Ronald K. Hawkins, February 2007–present
Brian R. Carrington, October 2009–present
Steven C. Wheelwright, October 2009–present
Scott C. Florence, January 2010–present

Church College of Hawaii/Brigham Young University–Hawai`i Presidents

Reuben D. Law, 1954–1958
Richard T. Wootton, 1958–1959 (acting); 1959–1964
Owen J. Cook, 1964–1971
Stephen L. Brower, 1971–1974
Dan W. Anderson, 1974–1980
J. Elliot Cameron, 1980–1986
Alton L. Wade, 1986–1994
Eric B. Shumway, 1994–2007
Steven C. Wheelwright, 2007–present

PCC Officers—2012

Von D. Orgill, President and CEO
P. Alfred Grace, Chief Operating Officer
Logoitino V. Apelu, VP—Operations
John Muaina Jr., VP—Human Resources
David C. Ralph, VP—Finance and CFO

PCC "Officer Team" Members—2012

Robert (Bobby) Akoi, Jr., Director—Protocol
  and Manager—Corporate Training
Freddie (Fred) J. Camit, Director—
  Management Information Systems and CIO
Orlin V. Clements, Director—Capital Projects
Keali`i Haverly, Director—In-Center Marketing
Raymond K. Magalei, Director—Marketing
Delsa S. Moe, Director—Cultural Presentations
Leslie (Les) Steward, Director—Physical Facilities
Fifita F. Unga, Director—Food and Beverage
J. Alan Walker, Director—Sales

PCC Senior Management Team–2012

Jay W. Akoi, Manager—Purchasing
Cy M. Bridges, Director—Artistic and Cultural Events
Seth K. Casey, Manager—Marketing
W. Halacy (Hal) Chu, Director—Compliance and Internal
  Controls
Ellen Gay Dela Rosa, Director—Theater
Tipa T. Galea`i, Manager—Guides
Francis A. Ho Ching, Assistant Director—Sales
Sally Mapu, Manager—Reservations
Fealofani (Losa) R. Moors, Manager—Food Production
Albert K. Nihipali, Manager—Asian Sales
Ali`imauofaleupolu (Ali1i) Toelupe, Manager—On-Site
  Group Services
Kathryn A. Tolleson, Manager—Compensation and
  Benefits
Branden J. Vendiola, Manager—Concessions
Matthew (Matt) L. Widman, Manager—Employment
Lawrence (Larry) H. Yuen, Controller

Glossary of Polynesian Words

(This expanded glossary is based on work originally done by R. Lanier Britsch)

Key to languages:
H—Hawaiian
F—Fijian
M—Māori
Mar—Marquesan
R—Rapa Nui (Easter Island)
S—Samoan
T—Tahitian
Ton—Tongan
P—Polynesian

`afa (S):** sennit cord made from coconut fiber. Also `aha (H); kafa (Ton)

ahu (R): altars on which moai were placed.

ahupua`a (H): section of land and sea that extended from the mountain top into the sea.

`ailao afi (S): the twirling of fire.

ali`i (H): chiefs, nobles.

aloha (H): love, mercy, compassion, pity. Also a greeting—hello, good-bye.

anuhe (M): edible fern

Aotearoa "Land of the Long White Cloud," modern Māori name for New Zealand.

`awapuhi kuahiwi (H): wild ginger. The slippery juice from the mature flower is used as a shampoo.

braguinha: Portuguese musical instrument prototype for the 'ukulele.

bula vinaka (F): greeting, hello or welcome; also "good health be with you always."

bure (F): house or hut.

bure kalou (F): god house or spirit house.

camakau (F): a style of outrigger canoe.

daru (F): sugarcane

derua (F): hollow bamboo tubes of various lengths, used as percussion instruments when struck on the floor.

esi (S): papaya.

fale fakatu`i (T): replica of Queen Salote's summer house in Tongan Village.

fau (T): wild hibiscus, used to make dancing skirts.

hā (H, M, P): breath, life force, spiritual power.

haka (M): war dance, posture dance.

haka manu manu (Mar): bird dance.

haka puaka (Mar): pig hunting dance.

halau (H): originally the hut for canoes, now known as a hula dance. It also means a school or a particular kumu (teacher) hula's dance troupe.

hale (H): house or building.
  cognates: fale (S), fare (T), vale (F).

hala (H): pandanus tree; its leaves are called lauhala and are woven into many useful things.

haole (H): a Caucasian, previously used to denote foreigners of any race.

hare vaka (R): stone house—Easter Island.

haupia (H): coconut pudding.

hei tiki (M): pendant in the form of a stylized human figure, usually of greenstone.

hiapo (Mar): cloth made from paper mulberry bark.

hikie`e (H): woven mattress or bed.

hongi (M): Māori greeting by touching foreheads and noses and exchanging hā, or breath.

hui (M): community gathering.

hui tau (M): annual gathering.

huki (H): to pull.

hukilau (H): to pull with lau, which are the leaves attached to fishing nets used to frighten the fish toward shore. Best known as Hawaiian community fishing.

hula (H): indigenous form of dance.

hula `auana (H): modern-style hula.

hula kahiko (H): ancient-style hula.

`ia ora na (T): greeting word similar to aloha.

`ili`ili (H): small flat stones used to make clicking rhythm as part of hula.

`ilima (H): a cherished flower for lei, commonly associated with Oahu.

imu (H): underground earth oven.

`iorana (R): greeting word similar to aloha.

Iosepa (H): Joseph; also a double-hulled canoe at the PCC named after Joseph F. Smith, fifth president of the LDS Church, known in Hawaii as Iosepa.

iwi (M): tribe.

kahili (H): feather standards of Hawaiian royalty.

kai (H): sea, ocean.

kalia (T): voyaging canoe.

kalo (H): taro.

kālua (H): pork steamed in an imu (earth oven).

kaoha (Mar): greeting similar to aloha in Hawaiian.

kauhale (H): the cluster of homes or buildings occupied by an `ohana, or family.

kapu (H): sacred and out of bounds.

cognates: tapu (P) and tabu. The English word *taboo* is derived from this term.

karanga (M): a woman's call of recognition as part of a formal greeting.

kava (P): shrub, member of the black pepper family. Roots produce a mildly narcotic substance used in drinks for social and religious ceremonies in Sāmoa, Tonga, Fiji, and Hawai`i.

keiki (H): child.

kia ora (M): greeting in Māori.

kika kila (H): steel guitar.

ko (H): sugarcane.

koa (H): mahogany trees. Useful for canoes, craving, furniture, etc.

komo mai (H): come in or join in.

konane (H): ancient Hawaiian form of checkers, played with pebbles.

koro (F): village.

koruru (M): carved face at the apex of the bargeboards of a whare.

kowhaiwhai (M): abstract painted curvilinear scroll patterns found on the ceiling beams of whare.

kukui (H): candlenut trees. Nuts were used for many purposes, especially to make lei and provide oil for lamps. State tree of Hawai`i.

kumala (T): sweet potato.

kumara (P, M): sweet potato.

kumu hula (H): hula teacher.

Kupe (M): discoverer of New Zealand.

kupuna (H): grandparent, ancestor, respected older generation.

Lā`ie (H): small town on the north shore

of O`ahu. Anciently a Pu`uhonua, a place of refuge; site of the PCC.

lau (H, S): leaves, usually sugarcane leaves for roof thatch and weaving, but also refers to the leaves of the pandanus tree.

lauhala (H): leaf of pandanus or hala tree, used for weaving and plaiting.

lavalava (S): men's wrapped skirt.

lei (H): garland or flower necklace.

lo`i (H): taro or rice paddy.

lomi (H): to squeeze, crush, or mash fine, as in lomi salmon.

lu`au (H): feast with traditional Hawaiian food.

lūu pulu (T): chicken, fish, or beef marinated in coconut milk, wrapped in young taro leaves, and steamed in an earth oven.

mahimahi (H): dolphin, a game fish popular for food.

mai`a (P): banana.

malae (S): grassy village green, center of Samoan villages.

malo e lelei (Ton): greeting.

mana (P): spiritual power, prestige, authority.

mana vai (R): agriculture enclosure to protect crops from wind.

manioka (S): tapioca.

maohi (T): the name Tahitians call themselves.

Māori (M): ordinary people, the indigenous people of New Zealand.

marae (M): the village common space in front of a meetinghouse.

masi (F): cloth made from paper mulberry bark.

mātai (F): craftsman

matai (S): chief, patriarch, or family head.

Maui (H): island of Hawai`i; also a Polynesian superman who fished islands up from the ocean floor.

moai (R): megalithic carved statues. The root of the word is similar to Hawaiian *mo`i*, indicating a person of highest rank.

moku (H): referred to both islands and districts within islands.

mu`umu`u (H): a loose-fitting dress developed in Hawai`i after missionaries came; a spinoff of the Mother Hubbard dresses or nightgowns popular on the mainland. Mu`umu`u means to be "cut off" and refers to the yoke that was omitted or cut off, and also the sleeves that were cut short.

nafa (T): skin-covered drums.

niu (P): coconut or young coconut.

O`ahu (H): the most populated island in the Hawaiian chain.

`ohana (H): family.

`ohe (H): bamboo. Varieties of this giant grass grow to three inches in diameter and fifty feet or more in height.

`ohi`a (H): a type of wood used for building.

ote`a (T): group dance form.

pa (M): village or settlement, formerly protected by palisades.

pareau (T): a wraparound dress, similar to a sarong.

papalangi (S): strangers, foreigners, or outsiders. Now shortened to palangi.

pia (P): Polynesian arrowroot. Provided the starch for thickening haupia (coconut pudding).

pili (H): a long, coarse grass used to thatch houses and huts.

poi (H): kalo prepared for eating in a mashed, pasty form.

poi (M): ball connected to a cord, used in some Māori dances.

polataufafo (S): blinds similar to Roman shades, hung in Samoan fale to provide protection from weather.

Polynesia: from Greek *poly*, meaning "many" and *nesos*, meaning "islands."

pounamu (M): loosely translated as greenstone or jade; New Zealand nephrite.

poupou (M): carved panels within a house, or whare.

pōwhiri (M): ritual greeting.

pua`a (H): pig.

pu`ili (H): split bamboo sticks used in the hula.

pukao (R): cylindrical red stone head adornments atop moai.

pu`uhonua (H): place of refuge.

Rapa Nui (R): Easter Island.

Rapanui (R): the indigenous Polynesian people of Easter Island.

ra ra (F): open grassy area between Fijian houses.

Rongorongo (R): the as yet unreadable script of Easter Island.

salusalu (F): Fijian-style lei.

savali ahi (S): the fire walk.

siva (S): dance.

siva naifi afi (S): fireknife dance.

siva o le fa`ataupati (S): slap dance.

ta`ata Tahiti (T): a name Tahitians use to refer to themselves.

tabua (F): ceremonial whale tooth.

taiaha (M): long fighting club, a carved lance.

taki (M): a leaf, sprig, or small woodcarving offered as part of the wero, the formal challenge to strangers who enter a Māori pa (protected village).

talofa (S): greeting, hello.

tamure (T): solo performance dance.

ta`ovala (Ton): a mat often made of woven pandanus leaves and tied as a skirt. Worn both for ceremonial and everyday clothing.

tapa (P): cloth made from the inner bark of the paper mulberry tree. Also **masi (F), ngatu (Ton).**

tapu (M, P): sacred and out of bounds, a religious restriction or constraint. Same as *kapu* in Hawaiian.

taro (P): a starchy food plant common throughout tropical Polynesia. **cognates: kalo (H), talo (S and Ton).**

tatau (T, P): tattoo.

tekoteko (M): carved figure that stands at the apex of a carved house.

ti (H): a woody plant with a stem supporting a large bunch of glossy leaves. The root is edible, and the leaves are used to create hula costumes.

tifaifai (T): Tahitian-style patchwork quilts.

tiki (P): image, statue, idol.

tohua (Mar): place of public assembly.

tofunga (R): consecrated class of stone carvers.

tufuga (Ton): a trade skills specialist.

`uala (H): sweet potato, believed to have originated in South America.

`ukulele (H): small four-stringed musical instrument; literally a "jumping flea."

`uli`uli (H): feathered gourd rattles to accompany hula dancing.

`ulu (H, S): breadfruit tree.

umala (S): yam.

`umu (P, Mar, S, Ton): above-ground oven; cook house or place of oven.

va`aalo (S): tuna fishing canoe.

vaka (Mar): canoe.

vale ni qase (F): house for older people.

voivoi (F): pandanus.

waka (F): war club made from a root.

waka (M): canoe.

waka taua (M): war canoe.

wauke (P): paper mulberry tree. Introduced around the islands by the Polynesian colonizers, paper mulberry is one of the most essential plants in the islands. The inner bark (bast) is the basis for tapa, Polynesia's cloth.

whare (M): house or hut.

whare runanga (M): house of learning or meeting house.

yaqona (F): kava drinking ceremony. Also **`ava (S), `awa (H).**

Notes

Chapter 1—Gathering Place

1. *Directory: Church of Jesus Christ of Latter-day Saints Hawaiian Mission*, April 1934, 10–11. Letter from Assistant Church Historian Andrew Jenson.

2. Britsch, *Moramona*, 54. Diary of Walter Murray Gibson, 5 November 1861.

3. Ibid., 63. Letter from Brigham Young in March 1865 to King Kamehameha V.

4. *Directory*, 24. Letter from Andrew Jenson, assistant Church historian to President Richard H. Wells, Pocatello, Idaho.

5. Moffatt, Woods, and Walker, 2.

6. An *ahupua`a* is an official Hawaiian division of land. Pie-shaped, it goes from its narrowest point in the mountains and broadens out down the hillside, finally reaching its widest dimension on the seashore and on into the sea. Those who live on an ahupua`a have the use of mountain, hillside, shore, and sea—every environment—for their benefit. From R. Lanier Britsch interview by Liz Thomas, 23 October 2003, Lā`ie, Hawai`i, transcript in PCC archives.

7. *Directory*, 24.

8. Law, 23–24. Recently, questions of authenticity were raised about the Lā`ie prophecy. A theory was put forth that Joseph F. Smith's words were actually directed to Iosepa, the Hawaiian colony in Utah's Skull Valley (1889–1917). An article to that effect was published by Harold S. Davis in *BYU Studies*. However, on 6 May 2010, R. Lanier Britsch, emeritus professor of history at BYU–Provo, who had originally questioned the provenance of the prophecy, issued a statement saying he had changed his mind after finding new information from an unpublished source confirming that the Lā`ie prophecy was well remembered and accepted in 1916. He concluded that Joseph F. Smith's Lā`ie prophecy was correctly named. Copy of Britsch's letter is in the PCC archives.

9. J. B. Musser in *Ka Elele O Hawaii*, the Hawaiian Mission Newsletter (1942): 17.

10. Britsch, *Moramona*, 121. William W. Cluff, early leader of the Hawai`i Mission, saw in vision President Brigham Young in Hawai`i and talked with him. President Young told him that "upon this land we will build a temple unto our God." President George Q. Cannon, who had been one of the first missionaries in Hawai`i in 1850, visited Hawai`i fifty years later and prophesied in both Lā`ie and Honolulu that the time would soon come when they would have a temple. In addition, Samuel E. Woolley, mission president and head of the Lā`ie Plantation (1895–1919), continually encouraged the Hawaiian Saints to gather their genealogies saying, "the time will come . . . that a temple will be built here."

11. Harold W. Burton as quoted by Edward L. Clissold, interview by R. Lanier Britsch, 1976, transcript in Church History Library.

12. The Church had been forced to abandon temples in Kirtland, Ohio, and Nauvoo, Illinois. Temples in St. George, Manti, Logan, and Salt Lake City, all in Utah, were dedicated before the turn of the twentieth century.

13. Britsch, *Unto the Islands of the Sea*, 153.

14. The Cardston Alberta Canada Temple, also outside the United States, was under construction at the time and was dedicated in 1923.

15. Lundwall, 155. In 1919, in the Lā`ie Temple dedicatory prayer, President Heber J. Grant included a special blessing for native Hawaiians. "We beseech thee, O Lord, that thou wilt stay the hand of the destroyer among the natives of this land, and give unto them increasing virility and more abundant health, that they may not perish as a people, but that from this time forth they may increase in numbers and in strength and in influence, that all the great and glorious promises made concerning the descendants of Lehi may be fulfilled in them."

Chapter 2—No Ordinary College

1. In the LDS Church, the term "General Authority" denotes members of the First Presidency and the Quorum of the Twelve Apostles, who have authority over all congregations and activities of the Church throughout the world.

2. Hugh J. Cannon was the son of George Q. Cannon, one of the first missionaries to come to Hawai`i in 1850.

3. Cannon, 57–58.

4. Law, 25.

5. Ibid., 28.

6. Ibid.

7. Some years later, Mary Jane Hammond would accompany her missionary husband to Lā`ie, Hawai`i. There she helped organized a school in Lā`ie, where David O. McKay participated in the 1921 flag-raising ceremony, and where he received the vision that would eventually result in Church College of Hawai`i/BYU–H.

8. As quoted in an undated biography of Edward L. Clissold, 9. Copy in PCC archives.

9. It has been said that Edward L. Clissold was one of the most influential and well-loved members of the Church in Hawai`i during the twentieth century. Over a fifty-year period, he served as a young missionary in Hawai`i, a counselor, and then as stake president of the Oahu Stake. He was president of the Lā`ie Temple three times, president of the Japanese/Central Pacific Mission, and twice president of the Hawaiian Mission. He was chairman of the board of Zion's Securities Corporation and the Pacific Board of Education for the LDS Church, as well as founding trustee and board member of CCH and the PCC. Recognized for his remarkable management skills and inspired spiritual leadership, Clissold's military (US Navy during World War I), civic, and Church service were characterized by his deep humility and unwavering obedience to the principles of the gospel. From undated biography of Edward L. Clissold.

10. Law, 56.

11. Middlemiss, 41.

12. Law, 64–65.

13. Ibid., 67.

14. Ibid.

15. Ibid., 69.

16. Wendell B. Mendenhall was born 30 September 1927 and filled a three-year mission to New Zealand, serving under President Matthew Cowley. While there he learned to speak Māori fluently. Later he served as stake president of the San Joaquin Stake in Stockton, California, and as president of the New Zealand Mission. He was called as chairman of the Church Building Committee in 1953, and as chairman of the Pacific Board of Education in 1957. He was responsible for the Labor Missionary Program, which built both the Church College of Hawai`i and the Polynesian Cultural Center.

17. O'Brien, 61.

18. Cummings, 267.

19. Ibid., 268.

20. Law, 256.

21. Ibid., 268.

Chapter 3—The Polynesian Cultural Center

1. Law, 119.

2. Matthew Cowley was born in Preston, Idaho, in 1897, but moved to Salt Lake City at the age of two months with his family when his father, Matthias F. Cowley, was called as an Apostle. When he returned to Utah from his first mission in 1919, he still had to complete high school. Soon he enrolled at the University of Utah, and after one year was admitted to the George Washington Law School in Washington DC, returning to Utah in 1926 to begin a law career.

3. Smith, 155.

4. Edward L. Clissold, interview by R. Lanier Britsch, 1976. Transcript in Church History Library, 20.

5. Ibid.

6. Miria Terauhina Rogers Tengaio, interview by Niki Wallace, 2 May 1997, BYU–H Oral History Program, Lā`ie, Hawai`i, transcript in PCC archives, 13.

7. With the overthrow of the Hawaiian monarchy in 1893, the hula lost its royal patronage and began to decline in popularity as a cultural practice and entertainment entity. This was particularly true of male hula, which did not totally disappear, but was only practiced on more remote areas of the islands. But when the hukilau began, male hula was included in the program and its popularity started to rise again. Alan Barcarse, a CCH student from Kaua`i, began dancing at the hukilau, instructed by Christina Nauahi. Later, Barcarse formed a troupe of other male dancers, including Ishmael Stagner, and began entertaining in Honolulu and Waikiki. Much Hawaiian culture was preserved in Lā`ie.

8. Kimball, 225.

9. Edward Clissold letter to President David O. McKay, 10 August 1961, copy in PCC archives.

10. Alice Pack, ed., *The Building Missionaries of Hawaii 1960–63* (Lā`ie, HI: privately printed, n.d.), 55. Copy in PCC archives.

11. Cummings, 298.

Chapter 4—Gathered in a Lo`i Kalo

1. William Kanahele, interview by Ken Baldridge, 3 June 1992, BYU–H Oral History Program, Lā`ie, Hawai`i, transcript in PCC archives.

2. Epanaia Whaanga (Barney) Christy, interview by Kalili Hunt, 18 June 1982, BYU–H Oral History Program, Lā`ie, Hawai`i, transcript in PCC archives.

3. Percy TeHira, in PCC interview, Lā`ie, Hawai`i, n.d., transcript in PCC archives.

4. Te Arohanui Māori was a group of 170 Māori in New Zealand who had been working in New Zealand as Church labor missionaries. On their off time, they spent time perfecting their cultural singing and dancing. Knowing that the PCC was being built, they saved enough money to pay their own way to Hawai`i for the dedication of the Center. See Chapter 5 for more of their story.

5. Mike Grilikhes, interview by R. Lanier Britsch and T. David Hannemann, 15 April 2003, Lā`ie, Hawai`i, transcript in PCC archives.

6. Rufus Neyemihyer, interview by Marcy Brown, 27 October 2003, Lā`ie, Hawai`i, PCC interview, transcript in PCC archives.

7. Thomas Murray, interview by Kalili Hunt, 8 July 1982, transcript in PCC archives.

8. Hugh B. Brown, talk and dedicatory prayer of the PCC, 13 October 1963, Lā`ie, Hawai`i, transcript in PCC archives.

9. Adamski, 3.

10. Ewing, 8.

Chapter 5—Polynesia in One Place

1. Oliver, 58.

2. Gordon B. Hinckley, address at PCC, Lā`ie, Hawai`i, October 2003, transcript in PCC archives.

Chapter 6—Night Show

1. Mike Grilikhes, interview by R. Lanier Britsch and T. David Hannemann, 15 April 2003, Lā`ie, Hawai`i, transcript in PCC archives.

2. Ibid.

3. Ibid. "We would come up to a problem and we'd say, brethren, down on your knees . . . and somebody would offer a prayer and we'd get up and say, okay, let's see how we can get this done."

4. Ibid.

5. Larry Nielsen, interview by T. David Hannemann and R. Lanier Britsch, 12 August 2003, Lā`ie, Hawai`i, transcript in PCC archives.

6. The upgraded IWork program replaced the IWES scholarship program, which was in place until the summer of 2009.

7. Debbie Hippolite Wright, PCC interview, October 2003, Lā`ie, Hawai`i, transcript in PCC archives.

8. Delsa Moe, interview by author, 6 May 2011, transcript in possession of author.

9. PCC guest e-mail, June 1, 2010.

Chapter 7—Road to Success

1. Meli Ulayawa Lesuma, n.d., transcript in PCC archives.

2. Salamasina Tuitama in Ellen Gay Dela Rosa, "Was It Destiny?" 13 July 2011, transcript in PCC archives.

3. "The Flop That Flipped," *Honolulu*, 12 October 1967.

Chapter 8—Foods and Feasting

1. Cy Bridges, PCC interview, October 2003, Lā`ie, Hawai`i, transcript in PCC archives.

2. Ibid.

Chapter 9—Welcoming the World

1. Von Orgill in Richard M. Romney, "Polynesian Cultural Center Celebrates 40 Years of Aloha," *Ensign* (October 2003), 75.

2. Les Moore, PCC interview, October 2003, Lā`ie, Hawai`i, transcript in PCC archives.

3. John Muaina, interview by T. David Hannemann, R. Lanier

Britsch, and Warren Bybee, 4 September 2003, Lā`ie, Hawai`i, transcript in PCC archives.

Chapter 10—Our Hearts Become One

1. Gordon B. Hinckley, address at PCC, October 2003, Lā`ie, Hawai`i, transcript in PCC archives.
2. Eric Shumway in Richard M. Romney, "Polynesian Cultural Center Celebrates 40 Years of Aloha," *Ensign* (October 2003), 74.
3. Law, 157.
4. Eric Shumway, PCC interview, October 2003, Lā`ie, Hawai`i, transcript in PCC archives.
5. Debbie Hippolite Wright, PCC interview, October 2003, Lā`ie, Hawai`i, transcript in PCC archives.
6. Cy Bridges, PCC interview, October 2003, Lā`ie, Hawai`i, transcript in PCC archives.
7. Marion G. Romney, dedicatorial address given BYU–H Aloha Center dedication, 26 January 1973, transcript in PCC archives.
8. Daniel Ng, PCC interview, October 2003, Lā`ie, Hawai`i, transcript in PCC archives.
9. Les Moore, PCC interview, October 2003, Lā`ie, Hawai`i, transcript in PCC archives.
10. Von Orgill, interview by author, 1 May 2011, Lā`ie, Hawai`i, transcript in possession of author.
11. Von Orgill in President's Message, *Imua Polenisi* 5 (October/November 2000), 3.

Sources

Books, Pamphlets, and Brochures

Ariyoshi, Rita. *All the Spirit of the Islands* (brochure). Lā`ie, HI: Polynesian Cultural Center of the Church of Jesus Christ of Latter-day Saints, 2003.

Ariyoshi, Rita. *Polynesian Cultural Center* (brochure). Santa Barbara, CA: Sequoia Communications, 1987.

Ariyoshi, Rita. *Polynesian Cultural Center: All the Spirit of the Islands* (brochure). Lā`ie, HI: PCC, 1995.

Britsch, R. Lanier. *Moramona: The Mormons in Hawaii*. Mormons in the Pacific Series. Lā`ie, HI: The Institute for Polynesian Studies, 1989.

———. *Unto the Islands of the Sea: A History of the Latter-day Saints in the Pacific*. Salt Lake City: Deseret Book, 1986.

Cannon, Hugh J. *David O. McKay around the World: An Apostolic Mission*. Provo, UT: Spring Creek Book Company, 2005.

Cummings, David W. *Mighty Missionary of the Pacific*. Salt Lake City: Bookcraft, 1961.

Directory: The Church of Jesus Christ of Latter-day Saints Hawaiian Mission. April 1934.

Faldmo, Norman W. Sr. ed. *Church College of Hawaii and Its Builders*, 1958 (yearbook).

Holmes, Tommy. *The Hawaiian Canoe*. 2nd ed. Honolulu: Limited Editions, 1993.

Kimball, Edward and Andrew E. Kimball Jr. *Spencer W. Kimball: Twelfth President of The Church of Jesus Christ of Latter-day Saints*. Salt Lake City: Bookcraft, 1977.

Law, Reuben D. *The Founding and Early Development of the Church College of Hawaii*. St. George, UT: Dixie College Press, 1972.

Lundwall, N. B., comp. *Temples of the Most High*. Salt Lake City: privately printed, 1941.

Middlemiss, Clare, comp. *Cherished Experiences from the Writings of President David O. McKay*. Salt Lake City: Deseret Book, 1955.

Moffat, Riley M., Fred E. Woods, and Jeffrey N. Walker. *Gathering to Lā`ie*. Mormons in the Pacific series. Lā`ie, HI: The Jonathan Napela Center for Hawaiian and Pacific Island Studies, 2011.

O'Brien, Robert. *Hands across the Water: The Story of the Polynesian Cultural Center*. Lā`ie, HI: Polynesian Cultural Center, 1983.

Oliver, Douglas. *Polynesia in Early Historic Times*. Honolulu: The Bess Press, 2002.

Rudd, Glen L. *Matthew Cowley Speaks: Discourses of Elder Matthew Cowley*. Salt Lake City: Deseret Book, 1954.

Pack, Alice C. ed. *The Building Missionaries in Hawaii*, 1963 (yearbook).

Smith, Henry A. *Matthew Cowley: Man of Faith*. Salt Lake City: Bookcraft, 1954.

Stagner, Ishmael W. *Kumu Hula: Roots and Branches*. Honolulu: Island Heritage Publishing, 2011.

Periodicals

Adamski, Mary. "Polynesians Flock to Laie to Create Culture Center." *Honolulu Star-Bulletin*, 5 October 1963.

"Ali`i Luau Opens to Rave Reviews." *Imua Polenisia* (PCC newsletter), July/August 1996.

Ewing, William H. "Let's Have No 'Coney Island.'" *The Honolulu Star-Bulletin*, 28 October 1963.

"The Flop that Flipped." *Honolulu*, 12 October 1967: 27.

"Food and Beverage Division Update." *Imua Polenisia*, October–November 1996: 4–5.

Glaus, Wayne. "Doctorate Recipient Provided Leadership in Building Campus." *Ke Alaka`i* 20 (10 January 1975). BYU–H in-house newsletter.

Imua Polynisia, October 2003 brochure.

Imua Polynisia 5 (October–November 2000), President's Message.

Ka Elele o Hawai`i 1942, Hawaiian Mission in Review (Hawaiian Mission newsletter, special edition, reprint 2005).

"Marketplace Update: An Overview of Hawaii Tourism Industry and PCC's Plans." *Imua Polenisia*, September 1996: 4–5.

Moe, Delsa. "*Festival of Arts*." *Imua Polenisia* (1996).

Moore, Lester C. "The Year in Review." *Imua Polenisia* 2 (January 1996).

"P.R.C. Premier Given Royal Welcome." *Ke Alaka`i* 29 (13 January 1984).

Riley, Robert. "Festival Polynesia's Success." *Los Angeles Times* 1 (September 1966): B–1.

Romney, Richard M. "Polynesian Cultural Center Celebrates 40 Years of Aloha." *Ensign*, October 2003: 74–75.

"Tofa My Feleni." *Imua Polenisia*, January 1996: 6.

"2011 Fireknife Competition at the Polynesian Cultural Center." *Honolulu Star Advertiser*, 6 May 2011.

Weaver, Sarah Jane. "A Place of Miracles: Polynesian Cultural Center Attracts Millions." *Church News*, 4 December 2010: 6–7.

Unpublished Manuscripts

Beebe, Fred G. *The Cluff Missionaries in the Sandwich Islands*. Copy in PCC archives.

Ferre, Craig. *A History of the Polynesian Cultural Center's Night Show 1963-1968*. (PhD dissertation, BYU, 1988). Copy in Church History Library, Salt Lake City.

Glaus, Wayne. *Polynesian Cultural Center Recollections* (April 2001). Unpublished transcript. Copy in PCC archives.